CAMINO WALK

CAMIN⊕ WALK

where inner & outer paths meet

MARIE-LAURE VALANDRO

LINDISFARNE BOOKS

2007

LINDISFARNE BOOKS

610 Main St., Great Barrington, MA 01230

www.lindisfarne.org

COVER IMAGE: "HANDMADE TWIG LAMP"
© ANITA—USED BY PERMISSION
COVER AND BOOK DESIGN: WILLIAM JENS JENSEN

"THE CALL OF THE WILD" BY ROBERT SERVICE (PUBLIC DOMAIN)
IMAGES BY THE AUTHOR—USED BY PERMISSION

LIBRARY OF CONGRESS CATALOGING-IN-PUBLICATION DATA

Valandro, Marie-Laure.
  Camino walk : where inner & outer paths meet /
Marie-Laure Valandro.
    p. cm.
  ISBN-13: 978-1-58420-052-9
  ISBN-10: 1-58420-052-9
  1. Valandro, Marie-Laure. 2. Spiritual biography.
3. Pilgrims and pilgrimages—Spain—Santiago de
Compostela. 4. Santiago de Compostela (Spain)—
Description and travel. I. Title.
  BL73.V345A3 2007
  263'.0424611—DC22

                              2007021774

Contents

The Call of the Wild

Robert Service

Have you gazed on naked grandeur where
　　there's nothing else to gaze on,
Set pieces and drop-curtain scenes galore.
Big mountains heaved to heaven, which the
　　blinding sunsets blazon,
Black canyons where the rapids rip and roar?
Have you swept the visioned valleys with the
　　green stream streaking through it,
Searched the Vastness for a something you have
　　lost?
Have you strung your soul to silence? Then for
　　God's sake go and do it;
Hear the challenge, learn the lesson, pay the
　　cost.

Have you wandered in the wilderness, the sage-
　　brush of desolation,
The bunch-grass levels where the cattle graze?
Have you whistled bits of ragtime at the end of
　　all creation,
And learned to know the desert's little ways?
Have you camped upon the foothills, have you
　　galloped o'er the ranges;
Have you roamed the air sun-lands through and
　　through?

Have you chummed up with the mesa? Do you
    know its moods and changes?
Then listen to the wild—it's calling you.

Have you known the Great White Silence, not a
    snow-gemmed twig aquiver?
(Eternal truths that shame our soothing lies?)
Have you broken trails on snowshoes? Mushed
    with your huskies up the river,
Dared the unknown, led the way, and clutched
    the prize?
Have you marked the map's void spaces, min-
    gled with the mongrel races,
Felt the savage strength of brute in every thew?
And though grim as hell the worst is, can you
    round it off with curses?
Then hearken to the Wild—it's wanting you.

Have you suffered, starved, and triumphed,
    groveled down, yet grasped at glory,
Grown bigger in the bigness of the whole?
"Done things" just for the doing, letting babblers
    tell their stories,
Seeing through the veneer of the naked soul?
Have you seen God in His splendors, heard the
    text that nature renders?
(You'll never hear it in the family pew.)
The simple things, the true things, the silent men
    who do things—
Then listen to the Wild—it's calling you.

They have cradled you in custom, they have
    primed you with their preaching,
They have soaked you in convention through
    and through;
They have put you in a showcase; you're a credit
    to their teaching—
But can't you hear the Wild?—it's calling you.
Let us probe the silent places, let us seek what
    luck betide us;
Let us journey to a lonely land I know.
There's a whisper on the night-wind, there's a
    star agleam to guide us,
And the Wild is calling, calling ... let us go.

CAMIN⊕ WALK

where inner & outer paths meet

AFTER MANY YEARS OF thinking about a longer walk, the opportunity finally comes. My daughter is in college, my son out of college, and my husband understands that I am not happy unless I go on journeys. Now I can take advantage of this new freedom by doing what I used to do before Children: travel everywhere on a shoestring budget. Whenever I'd had enough cash saved up from my teaching in various places I would invariably fly somewhere and take long walks to feel the land, visit sacred sites, learn people's customs, religions, foods, languages, and so on. (I did not know then that I could have made a living doing just that.) Looking back, I see that, in all these seemingly random journeys, I visited many sacred places scattered around the earth. Now the Camino was calling, and I had to answer; fortunately, it wasn't so far away.

In the telling of the outward journey, I will mention many philosophers, poets, scholars, modern alchemists, Buddhist masters, scientists such as Rudolf Steiner, Georg Kühlewind, Dennis Klocek, Christopher

Bamford, Goenkaji, and many others, living and dead, who have been my companions for so many years through books and living words that helped shape my inner journey. Without these great guides, I would not be who I am today. We all know that there is no outer path without the inner path.

In April, two weeks before I left, I was agonizing over whether I should go. After going through a guilt trip and getting nowhere in my deliberations, I stepped into action mode. I ordered a women's backpack and helped myself to some clothes from my daughter's National Outdoor Leadership School (NOLS) hiking trip to Patagonia. There I was, saying goodbye to husband, family, friends, and kids. I was off to France to begin my walk in Saint-Jean-Pied-de-Port for six weeks of rambling through mountain paths, forests paths, paths with lovely edges, farm fields, valleys, rocky hills, red-earth paths, ancient Roman roads, endless arid plateaus, soft green hills, sweet smelling soft paths, moorland, forgotten rocky paths in mountainous regions, busy highways, big cities, and villages. Here the words of Thoreau seem appropriate, from Jim Vickery's *Wilderness Visionaries:*

> As a walker Thoreau remained a pilgrim, having met but one or two persons in his life who understood the art of walking, who had a genius for sauntering. A true walker, Thoreau said in his essay, requires a direct dispensation from heaven. As for himself, he couldn't at age thirty-four stay in his chamber for a single day without acquiring some rust. He stressed the importance of being

awake to one's senses and that in his own walks at least he tried to shake off his morning occupations and obligations to society. It wasn't always easy to rid himself of the village, however, for the thought of some work would run in his head and he would not be where his body was. He would be out of his senses. What he wanted to do during his walks was *return* to his senses.

"What business have I in the woods," he asked himself, "if I am thinking of something out of the woods?"

Then abruptly, as if he realized the connection between his sauntering and insight (the latter dependent on the former), he extolled wildness. From it come "the tonics and barks which brace mankind." The best literature is rooted in the wild, he said, and civilization needs wilderness to keep its strength and proper perspective. He cited the story of Romulus and Remus being suckled by a wolf as not being a meaningless fable but as an allegory of how the founders of any state that rises to eminence are nourished and invigorated by similar wild sources (p. 36).

To preserve wild animals, Thoreau realized, generally implies the creation of a forest in which they can dwell. So it is with human beings. He did not want every person or every part of a person cultivated, no more, anyway, than he wanted every acre of earth cultivated; part should be tilled, but the greatest part should be meadow and forest. It was the wildness in human beings and their naturalness and instinctive oneness with ecosystems that Thoreau feared was disappearing. Nature informs humanity when her wild animals are becoming extinct, he said, but not when the wild *man* in her does. He bemoaned how, early in life, people are weaned from nature; "this vast, savage, howling mother of ours...lying all around, with such beauty, and such affection for her children." Instead, there is only society and culture, and exclusive interaction of person on person, a web of social heading for a speedy end.

"Walking," however, ended characteristically with a hop toward hope. All good things, Thoreau concluded, are wild and free, and in wildness is the preservation of the world. There will come a time, moreover, when a "great awakening light, as warm and serene and golden as on a bankside in autumn," will illumine "our hearts and minds."[1]

Like everyone on this kind of journey, I worried about such things as crossing the Pyrenees in cold weather. In reality, however, I was worried more about what I would find out about myself than I was anything else. I was really on a journey of self-renewal. Like all women of my age (in our fifties, that is), we have many still-unanswered questions. The years of procreation are left behind, and men-o-pause has passed. Now we are supposed to enter the years of wisdom. I read

---

1. Jim Dale Vickery, *Wilderness Visionaries: Leopold, Thoreau, Muir, Olson, Murie, Service, Marshall, Rutstrum,* Minocqua, WI: NorthWord Press, 1994, p. 37.

somewhere that when we can no longer bear children, that energy becomes available for spiritual work. Other questions, however, begin to take shape. What should I really do now that my children are independent? When children like mine depart, they leave an awful lot of energy available. What is the meaning of love when you have raised your children, and when you and your husband take yourselves for granted? I would ponder such questions during this journey. I would also meditate everyday on being grateful for everything that comes my way—people, scenery, weather, or anything. I was to be in that mood for the whole time, as a kind of prayer mood for this pilgrimage.

I had walked before, in the Himalayas, India, the Middle East, Greece, the Andes, Ecuador, the Machu Pichu Trail in Peru, the Canadian Rockies, Alaska, New England, Patagonia, and many other beautiful settings, but those walks did not hold the aura of this pilgrimage. This was, after all, a Christian pilgrimage hundreds of years old; it had seen hundreds of thousands of Christian pilgrims on its path. The others are also ancient pilgrimages, but this one is a Christian path.

One must be prepared for transformation on a pilgrimage. Whether one is aware of it or not, transformation will happen. It is better, of course, to be ready for changes, which allows them to happen more easily. Isn't this the reason for a long pilgrimage? By leaving our natural surroundings, we take the first step, which opens one to the world and what it offers. We make a space. The twenty-first century makes it difficult for us to make that space by wishing to fill it up. Mostly what fill us up does not make us healthy. To create this space, it must be empty, which can be a very painful process.

With a mostly empty backpack and roaming empty paths, it becomes easier to empty oneself of the nonessential and fill the space with what counts. For many, it is the first experience of what it means to have space. Many pilgrims are older women who have devoted their lives to others for many years, while never taking time to claim a space for themselves. Now was the time. For men who had worked hard all their lives to take care of family, it was time to reconsider everything and be alone to feel the new space.

> AUM
> Seek the path.
> Seek the path by going deep within your self.
> Seek the path by going boldly out of your self.

The last two sentences seem to contradict each other. In truth, they express two extraordinary facts. Turning inward is the first half of a path. To begin with, at the present stage of development, human beings are living *in* their sense perception of the external world. Even when they use their intellect and understanding to process these sense impressions, they remain "outside." When people free themselves from the sense impressions and withdraw into themselves, they still have the power to think. This thinking is then emptied of external contents, which signifies "going deep within the soul." Precisely because thinking is "emptied," new content can flow from within. This content is spiritual, just as the previous content was sensory. Because of this, however, human beings can then step out of themselves. One can step out of the sphere of the lower self and into the "spiritual external world." This is indicated by the sentence "Seek the path by going boldly out of yourself."

A mystic combines all these sentences with the syllable "AUM." The *A* signifies the firm grip on the state, or condition, in which human beings always find themselves at their present stage of evolution. The *U* is a symbol for going deep within, and the *M* signifies stepping out into the spiritual external world."[1]

🌀

My flight was uneventful. Heathrow Airport was the biggest mess ever. I lost my chance to see Turner's paintings at the museums, because so many people waited in line. The train rides in France were fun, and, having finally found a place to sleep the previous night in Bayonne around midnight, I arrived in the small town of Saint-Jean-Pied-de-Port by ten o'clock on a beautiful morning.

When I arrived at the St. John's office (the friends of pilgrims' office) to get my pilgrim's passport in Saint-Jean-Pied-de-Port, the man working there offered me a job as a volunteer, because I was trying to help people

1. Rudolf Steiner, *Esoteric Lessons 1904–1909: From the Esoteric School*, Great Barrington, MA: SteinerBooks, 2007, Berlin Oct. 4, 1904, p. 33.

who did not speak French or Spanish. It was tempting and I kept it in mind in case I wanted to spend more time in this quaint village. As a few of us waited, we were given a *coquille St. Jacques* to hang on the back of our packs, as well as a pilgrim's passport so that we could get reasonable prices (five to eight euros) at all the hostels for pilgrims. I never knew why they called these beautiful shells *"coquille St. Jacques"* in the French restaurant in Boston, where I had worked to put myself through college. Why "Saint Jacques"? Now I realized that it had nothing to do with food; the shell was adopted by all the pilgrims, and St. James is often seen with the shell and a staff in sculptures. Pilgrims returned home with shells from the seashore at the end of their pilgrimage in Finistère (end of the earth), where we find the famous "coquilles St. Jacques."

> The cockle shell or pilgrim's shell is the most characteristic attribute of the pilgrimage to Santiago de Compostela. All pilgrims have worn it over the centuries and it appears on the images of the saint in his robe as pilgrim which have appeared as sculptures, prints, and paintings. It is also a symbol found on facades, altarpieces, coats of arms, and objects related to the city, its cathedral, pilgrimage and the Apostle. For medieval pilgrims, the shell was a sort of certificate to prove that they had undertaken the pilgrimage. The cockle shell was a very common shellfish in the region, collected on its beaches and along the rocky coastline and on their return home they would sew it onto their clothes, a visible witness to the fact that they

had reached this spot where the Apostle was buried in the corner of far west Europe. Many aspects of the pilgrimage have evolved over the years, but some items of pilgrims' clothes have remained the same. They still wear the cockleshell attached to their staff or sewn onto their rucksacks or clothes. In the past, as we see in numerous images found in villages along the pilgrimage Route, the shell was also attached to the wide-brimmed hat that pilgrims wore to protect themselves from the sun, cold, and rain. Other standard items of clothing were an overcoat or cape that was short so as not to hinder walking, another small leather cape that covered the shoulders and arms, and the characteristics long, metal-tipped staff from which hung a variety of objects including the gourd which was used as a water bottle. The notches made on the staff by hostel keepers along the way indicated the numbers of nights that a pilgrim has spent in each place."[1]

I set off around ten in the morning of April 21. I decided to make the trip over the pass, because of wonderful weather and because I would stay halfway at the Refuge-Auberge d'Orisson, about nine kilometers ahead. I walked with an English man who generously offered to carry some of my stuff. As usual, I was overloaded. It was great to get into the rhythm of walking with nothing to do but enjoy the scenery as we climbed steadily into the hills. It is a fairytale landscape, with

1. Maria Unceta, *La Catedral de Santiago de Compostela*, Spain: Aldeasa, 2004, p. 15.

little farms dotting the lower Pyrenees Mountains. It is spring, so they are busy sheering the sheep, and we hear the mothers bleating, upset without their lambs. Cream-colored, large cows gently graze, and the fields are lovingly tended. Everywhere is a beautiful spring green. In the town, I bought my favorite things from France ... wonderful sheep cheese, pâté, and artisanal chocolates, which tastes better as you feel the touch of the artisan who made it. I felt bad that I could not stay in this lovely town for a while

The walk up into the lower hills is arduous; it is hot and I am sweating and a bit tired, because I have not slept much since leaving Chicago. We walk slowly on the small road past several farms along the way. The first days are excruciating; as we climb I slow down and concentrate on putting one foot ahead of the other. The backpack hurts, everything hurts, but there is nowhere to go but up—slowly and patiently, allowing my body to become accustomed to this new burden. Thoughts come into my mind, questioning my sanity. My body asks, why are you doing this to yourself? My mind ignores the question, encouraged by the scenery and these ancient, sacred paths. How wonderful to get back to the essence of things. Yes, I have legs and a back, and they were meant to take me places and carry things, not to sit and be *taken* somewhere. That means effort and pain until the muscles get used to the new strains. It usually takes about five days.

Eventually, we arrived at the little *albergue,* or hostel, run by a Basque family. They had Basque music playing, and as a linguist I have always been curious about the origin of this very ancient language, which

*First day in Saint-Jean-Pied-de-Port to receive
"credentials" allowing me to stay in pilgrims' lodgings*

remains a great puzzle to many scientists. Hearing the
songs in this ancient language takes one to a faraway
land. The great scientist Arnold D. Wadler has been
shedding some light on these mysteries, and I quote him
extensively to entice people to read the book itself:

> Now we return to the Basques, and to the evi-
> dence of their connection with the people of the
> British Isles. Let us keep in mind that the Basques
> today have survived in the territory of the Pyrenees
> Mountains on the Hispano-French border. Their

tongue is the most ancient witness of unrecorded European history, related with Egyptians and North-African languages on the one hand and with the dialects of the Caucasus on the other. The grammatical structure of their venerable speech is strikingly similar to American Indian idioms connections with the West—across the Atlantic—and to the East with African and Asiatic tongues. The Basque people are descendants of the Hibernian nation which gave Spain and Portugal the name of the Hibernian peninsula and had founded and carried on the so-called Hibernian Mystery centers for thousands of years in the lands extending along the shores of the Atlantic Ocean in Western Europe from Hibernia to the Hebrides and doubtless beyond.

Were the Basques always compressed in that narrow corner which is called the Basque country today, or did they once extend far beyond it, and in which directions? In Latin and in Spanish their name is *Vascon-es*.... The French province extending north of the Pyrenees on the shores of the Atlantic is called *Gascogne,* or *Guascogne,* which again means the *land of the Basques*. Thus we arrive almost as far as Bordeaux in reconstructing the ancient home of the oldest nation in Europe. This conclusion, drawn from linguistic facts, is easily supported by archeological evidence: the Franco-Cantabrian caves, which, like the American Indians *Kivas* and many caves in early epochs, were Mystery Centers and religious gatherings places. More geographical evidence is offered by the name of the *Biscayan,* or *Viscayan Gulf,* marking the extension of the territory once peopled by the Basques up to the northwestern tip of Brittany and France, to the English Channel. Here the Basques must have come into contact with the most ancient natives of England at a time long before the Celtic invasion of the East. We could call this region the western contact-zone.

Yet there is an eastern contact-zone as well which again can be proved by language. There was a time when the Basques extended over all France, before even the Gauls had arrived from the Orient. The mountain-chain which separates France and Germany, the *Vosges,* was called in Latin VOSEG-US MONS (Vosges Mountain), and in modern German die *Vogesen.* Yet in the oldest German records such as *Walthari-Lied* (Walter's Song) this barrier was still named *Wasgen-Wald* or Wasgen Forest. This old name *Wasgen-* is so assonant to *Vasgon-es* that we cannot but see in it the name of the Basques. *Wasgen-Wald is literally Basque Forest.* The Basques without any doubt once extended as far as Germany and probably deep into Central Europe. This was in an epoch long before the landing of the Celts, The Romans, the Anglo-Saxons in the British Isles.[1]

---

1. Arnold D. Wadler, *One Language: Source of All Tongues,* Great Barrington, MA: Lindisfarne Books, 2006, pp. 41–42.

Here is another connection from the same source that runs into the much more distant past:

The Canary Islands extend toward the West similar to the Azores. The Last vestiges of the Guanche language, some hundred words in all, have been preserved by some British and Spanish scholars. They show a certain connection with the North African tongues, Berber, Hamitic, and Old Egyptian. Schuchardt-Graz, Nikolai Barr and other linguists have proven this side of their relationship, and also their affinity with the Basque tongue. The Basque vocabulary is close to the Hamito-Semitic family of tongues, while its grammar is related with the American Indian dialects. This fact is characteristic not only of Basque but of other related idioms and may be illustrated by one example, the title *NEG-us* of Abyssinia. We find its relatives in Basque *NAG-ushi* (prince), Hebrew *NOG-esh* (ruler), and Hindoo books mention *Deva NAH-ushi* as a ruler of the universal empire of the Atlantean extending beyond the pillars of Hercules and deep into the Mediterranean basin, to Hellas in the North, and the Egyptian border in the south.

Basque NAG-ushi (Prince) a Link with Africa and Asia

Atlantis	Europe, Basque	Africa, Abyssinia
NAH-ushi	NAG-ushi	NEG-us
(emperor)	(prince)	(emperor)
Asia, Hebrew		Mongolian
NOG-esh		NOY-on
(ruler)		(chief)

This old title is a short form of *INC-a,* Greek *ANAK-s* (ruler, prince), the post-diluvian name *INACH-os,* the *NOAH* of the Bible. It shows the deep connection of the Hibernian center of culture with other parts of the world. What however is of a far greater interest to us, is to know whether Guanche actually connects the East and West, the Old with the New world....

Guanche CEL (SEL) and Other Related Moon-names.

America, Peru	Guanche	Europe, Basque
KILL-a	CEL	HILL
(moon)	(moon)	(moon)
Africa, Bantu		Asia, Arabic
EYEL-i		HIL-al
(moon)		(moon)
		(Ibid., pp. 189–192)

With just these few examples, we can see how ancient the Basque language is. Arnold Wadler goes on to mention hundreds of examples of these links between the hemispheres and the lost continent that existed between the Americas and Europe.

◈

We certainly felt the sacredness of these mountains. It was still early afternoon when we settled into our first cramped quarters, so we all sat on the terrace overlooking the valleys and the western sky, many in deep thought, pondering the long journey we would all undertake. We sat all afternoon and evening chatting, some drinking enormous amount of beer, others coffee or other drinks. Around seven o'clock that evening, we enjoyed a communal dinner that included Canadians, English, Germans, Swedish, French, Spaniards, Austrians, and Japanese. With lots of red wine flowing at supper, we had some very lively discussions about religion, Catholics, faith, atheism, and people who try to find a reason to believe in something. These words of Rudolf Steiner come to my mind:

> What do we now have? People all want to be their own lord; egotism and self-seeking have been carried to the extreme. A time is coming when no other authority will be recognized than one that people accept voluntarily, one whose power is based on voluntary trust. Those mysteries founded on the power of the Spirit are called the "Mysteries of the Spirit." Those that will be based in future on a foundation of trust, on the power of trust, are called the "Mysteries of the Father." We will conclude our culture with those mysteries. This new impulse, the power of trust, must come; otherwise we are heading toward a splintering, toward a universal cult of the self and egotism.[1]

In the dinner discussion, most people enjoyed the sharing of the others' beliefs. In the atmosphere of the people assembled there, one could feel the deep enjoyment in hearing one another's stories. Different languages were spoken at different ends of the table,

---

1. Rudolf Steiner, *The Christian Mystery: Early Lectures,* Hudson, NY: SteinerBooks, 1998, p. 180.

and one could partake in one language or the other. However, we all had one language in common, the one that had brought us together from all parts of the globe for the next few weeks as we walked the Camino.

No one wants to believe in the one abstract god—or three gods or two anymore. People are trying in general to find a faith that is more opened to that of others, an "à la carte" religion. The days of the holy doctrine, the pope, rabbis, priests, pastors, or mullahs, are over for many. We are on a new page, searching for something new and rewriting everything each day. Rudolf Steiner put it this way:

> What, in effect, is theology? A knowledge of God imposed from without under the form of dogma, as a kind of supernatural logic. And what is Theosophy [or Anthroposophy]? A knowledge of God which blossoms like a flower in the depth of the individual soul. God, having vanished from the world, is reborn in the depths of the human heart.[1]

As I said earlier, one of the reasons for going was to be thankful everyday for everything, good and bad; that was to be my daily practice. This practice would lead me to live in the moment, which was the other component. To be thankful and to be present to everyone and everything, while quieting all the intellectual stuff so that I could feel with my heart instead of my head. I am trying to work on that new muscle

---

1. Rudolf Steiner, *An Esoteric Cosmology,* Blauvelt, NY: Garber, 1987, p. 20.

of the heart by removing anxieties as they come along.
Rudolf Steiner:

> It is the same with feelings of anxiety. They have
> no place today and will have still less in the future.
> What occurs when we feel anxious? The blood is
> driven back into the center of the human being,
> and into the heart, in order to form a firm central
> point and make the human being strong in oppo-
> sition to the outer world. It is the inmost power
> of the "I" which does this. This power of the "I,"
> which affects the blood, must become ever stron-
> ger and more conscious;... what is harmful and
> unnatural today, however, is the feeling of fear
> which is connected with this flow of the blood.
> In the future that must no longer be so; only the
> power of the "I" without fear must be active.

> Throughout human evolution, the outer world
> becomes ever more antagonistic toward us. You
> must learn, increasingly, to set your inner strength
> against this outer world that presses upon you.
> But anxiety must vanish; it is especially necessary
> for anyone who proceeds with an esoteric train-
> ing to free himself from all feelings of fear and
> anxiety. Anxiety only has a certain justification
> in making us aware that we need to make our-
> selves strong, but all unnatural feelings of anxiety
> which torment the human being must disappear
> altogether.... Anyone in the future who does not
> rid himself here of the habit of anxiety will there
> fall into one dreadful terror after another....

Our contemporary culture is itself creating those horrifying monsters which will threaten the human being on Jupiter [the far future]. You need only look at the huge machines which human technology is today constructing so ingeniously. The human being is creating demons for himself which in the future will rage against him. Everything that he builds today in the way of technical appliances and machines will assume life in the future and oppose him in terrible enmity. Everything that is created for mere utility to satisfy individual or collective egoism will be the human being's enemy of the future. We are today far too concerned with gaining useful advantage from what we do. If we really wish to help advance evolution, we should not be concerned with the usefulness of something but with whether it is beautiful and noble. Our actions should not be guided only by utility but by our pure delight in what is beautiful. Everything created by the human being to satisfy his artistic needs, in pure love of beauty, will assume life in the future and contribute to his higher evolution.... Everything beautiful and noble that we cultivate today leads to a strengthening of the good on Jupiter; everything that occurs as a result of egoism and utility leads to a strengthening of the bad.

In order for the human being to become equal to facing the evil powers of the future, he must take hold of the inmost strength of his "I." He must be consciously able to regulate the blood in such a way that it makes him strong in the face of evil, but wholly without anxiety. He must have in his power the strength to direct the blood inward.[1]

With such weighty meditations, I began the pilgrimage like everyone else.

That evening many people were turned away because there was no room and, after a three-hour climb, they had to go back down or sleep in a lean-to under the stars in some meadow. This thankfulness goes a long way in dissipating everything, giving one strength to go on when it seems impossible. Anxiety cannot survive this simple attitude.

I had been warned by friends who had walked the Camino, and I had read about the nasty dogs along the way, so I was ready to meet them if or when they came.

Before setting off the next morning, I lightened my backpack by leaving behind at least three pairs of socks, some underwear, and other things. That night we experienced a beautiful sunset in indigos and carmines over distant mountains. My afternoon walking partner (who drank at least ten pints and a couple of bottles of red wine) took off in the morning before sunrise. Those English men sure can drink and walk.

Hiking in the morning was a bit cold, with a biting wind that required gloves, a hat, and a jacket. The wind was so strong that at times we all felt that we might be blown off the path. I was still getting used to my backpack and my shoulders were sore. I left at eight in the morning with a group of French travelers, whose

1. Rudolf Steiner, *Guidance in Esoteric Training: From the Esoteric School,* London: Rudolf Steiner Press, 2001; lecture in Munich Jan. 16, 1908, pp. 111–113.

leader was at least seventy-five and going twice as fast as me. Of course, she had a very small pack. I stopped to look at the views and ate an apple and some sheep cheese. There are places along the way to sit and medi-tate with a statue of the Virgin or the Cross. The views are magnificent while hiking on mountains as high as 4500 feet. One can still see little farms probably used only during the summer; this is Basque country. There is a special smell to the air up here. Is it excitement, or joy? The French word *ennivrement* is perfect ... intoxi-cated by the views. I stop all the time, which makes it much slower. There are pee stops, drinking stops, rear-ranging-the-pack stops, snacks, stops for removing or adding clothes, and resting stops, all while watching the enchanting views everywhere. We passed a herd of wild horses—mares with their colts galloping on the high mountains, meadows, and moorland, grazing or sleeping on the grass. They are beautiful and belong to this wilderness. It feels like Ireland or Scottish moors, and climbing higher, farms are no longer visible; it is too cold and wild. There are primitive, stone enclo-sures for people to rest in if they are stuck up here in raging elements.

The wind picked up to at least thirty-five miles per hour against us, so it was a real struggle to get going. We had to carry heavy packs uphill, against this rag-ing wind, but it was not raining so we were lucky. I walked with a couple of Brazilians, who stopped regu-larly like me. They were not racing over the Camino like many others. We passed into Spain and the province of Navarre. We walked up and down the side of a moun-tain and then finally went down toward Roncevalle.

These words, born in these mountains, come to mind:

La Chanson de Roland

> Roland sent bien que la mort l'entreprend,
> Que de la tête au coeur elle descend.
> Dessous un pin il court, encore alerte;
> La face au sol, s'etend sur l'herbe verte;
> Pose sous lui son cor et son épée;
> Vers les paiens tient la tête tournée.
> S'il fait ainsi, le preux, c'est qu'il entend
> Que Charles dise avec toute sa gent;
> "Le gentil comte est mort en conquérant."
> Battant sa coulpe et puis la rebattant,
> Pour ses péchés il offert a Dieu son gant.
>
> (STANZA CLXXIV)

"La Chanson de Roland" is both the oldest and the best of the extant *chansons de geste*. It is one of a group that celebrates the prowess of the Emperor Charlemagne (742–814) and his courtiers. It was composed around 1100 by an unknown *trouvère* and is based on an authentic event: the defeat in 778 of Charlemagne's rear guard at Roncesvalles in the Pyrenees. Briefly, the story is this: Charlemagne has taken all of Spain from the Saracens, except for the realm of Marsile, king of Zaragoza (then called Saragossa). Aided by the treachery of Ganelon (stepfather of the hero Roland), Marsile makes a deceptive peace and then falsely falls upon the French rear guard commanded by Roland as it returns northward to France through the Pyrenees. Roland can summon Charlemagne's main body to his aid by blow-

Where Inner & Outer Paths Meet 🌸 33

ing his horn, his *olifant*. Regarding such an appeal as cowardly, he refuses to do so until it is too late. By wreaking frightful destruction on the Saracens, all the French are killed, Roland last. Summoned by the dying Roland's blast, Charlemagne frightens away the enemy. Ganelon is judged and executed, together with a number of his relatives.[1]

This particular place is so rich in history that I could not help but try to make it come alive and this poem of Roland is so much part of this area. It was a name I had heard so often during my schooling in France. All the pilgrims who walk through the area try to live in these events. The great human beings who brought so much to humanity leave a kind of residue wherever they have been. To perceive it, one must be sensitive to what lives in these places. Provided we have made a space for these feelings to enter, walking alone helps us live into this dimension.

> A great pilgrimage path must be viewed in connection with the country and the continent through which it passes. In Spain, we stand upon an ancient piece of earth. According to old maps drawn from clairvoyant insights (and to which Rudolf Steiner referred), this place existed as early as the Lemurian time (in the far distant past, before the time of Atlantis). Curiously, a small strip of land in North America—present-day California—also existed during the Lemurian

---

1. Morris Bishop & Kenneth T. Rivers, *A Survey of French Literature, vol. 1: The Middle Ages and the Sixteenth Century,* New York: Harcourt Brace Jovanovich, 1965.

period. People familiar with both Spain and California are always struck by the similarity of their landscapes; it is more than a coincidence that California was settled by Spaniards.

We know that, as a harbor, Cádiz was a busy trading port at the end of the Atlantean period. The Old Testament refers to Cádiz, much later around 1200 BCE, as one of the most important trade and distribution centers. In Spain, the effects remain of two great mystery centers: the Jupiter Mysteries in northern Spain and the Venus Mysteries in the south. Both worked their way into the spiritual history of pre-Christian and, especially, Christian Spain.

Spain looked quite different then. During Roman times, it was said that a squirrel could hop from Biscay to Gibraltar without touching the ground. Great forests covered the countryside through which the Romans built their first roads. Ancient, sacred Atlantean spirituality lived in these forests. Rudolf Steiner speaks repeatedly of the spirituality in which the people of Lemuria and Atlantis felt the landscape as part of the constitution of their own being. They did not experience their body as in here and nature as out there. They experienced body and nature as one. Steiner notes that remnants of this consciousness are preserved, for example, in Australia—part of the old Lemurian continent—by its aboriginal inhabitants. He called them the very last Lemurians. We know that they can sense a water source a hundred kilometers away, or that they sense distant food as if it belongs to their body. This same experience is found with the natives of North America. The song of a Native American chief, astonished that white people wanted to buy land, says: How can someone buy the land? It is our brother! The wind cannot be bought either; it, too, is our brother. Nor water, for it is our sister. In this way, up through the nineteenth century, this Atlantean attitude lived on in Native Americans in North America. Nature is brother and sister. Such an attitude also resounds in the Camino and works through it into the situation in Europe.[1]

🌸

I walked past a beautiful old birch forest with marshland at the bottom. Old imposing buildings then came into view. One used to be a hospital for the pilgrims. Upon entering, one could smell the strong odor of ether; it must be impregnated into the walls. Sadly, however, the place no longer has real life but died many centuries ago. The old stones have seen much, but they are now silent and overgrown. As you walk in these areas, however, you can feel a certain tense, foreboding atmosphere—not the place for a family picnic.

In this small town I was reminded of pilgrims who often died on the way or who were gravely ill, so that

---

1. Manfred Schmidt-Brabant & Virginia Sease, *Paths of the Christian Mysteries: From Compostela to the New World,* London: Temple Lodge, 2003, pp. 83–84.

hospitals had to be built to treat them. Along the path we saw several crosses with the names of pilgrims who had died recently on their way to Santiago. Travelers often think of the souls who came here to die, making the land of the dead closer to us, or making the dead actually part of the living. Most of the pilgrims are touched by seeing these crosses, and we are reminded of our short stay on this earth and how we must make the most of it.

As soon as I arrived I had a cup of delicious coffee to get warmed up and met up with two other women. We decided to share a room instead of sleeping in the large and cold hostel for pilgrims, which had a huge room that could accommodate at least 120 pilgrims.

My companions for the night were a French woman who had been walking already for at least six weeks; she had come from Vézelay, the well-known Marian site, dedicated to Mary Magdalene in France and a destination for many pilgrims during the Middle Ages. She was already halfway and had walked 800 kilometers (about 500 miles), and we were just beginning. The other woman was a Canadian who was mourning the loss of her much-loved husband. She had come to be closer to him and to meditate and heal. He had been a catholic priest before they fell in love and married.

We shared a lovely meal, happy to be eating and not have to prepare it—a luxury for me after so many years of cooking for my family. Everyone was thrilled to be on the walk; our faces bronzed by the wind, we relaxed for the evening and just enjoyed being ourselves.

We left Roncesvalles around nine the next morning, following a great breakfast. It was a luxury, because when you stay in the albergue, the hostel for pilgrims, you must be out by before seven o'clock, leaving without food because nothing is open at that hour. The other pilgrims had already gone on ahead of us.

As we walk through another nice beech forest and through small villages, I grow accustomed to the backpack. Before starting a gentle climb into softer hills, we filled our water bottles at a village fountain with water coming from the mouths of beautiful lions. The meadows were full of mares and their colts, farms with milking cows, people still living with the rhythm of the land. We were traversing meadows, farmers' fields, and forests, all lively with farming activities. Tractors ready to work the fields, and red-faced peasants walking to their barns to milk the cows.

Violets were starting to bloom and flowers that I have not seen since I was child growing up in the Dijon hills. I used to love the cuckooflowers—little yellow bellflowers with their long stems dotting the side of the path. Birds were singing everywhere, and one could see newborn foals resting in the soft grass. Signs of spring were everywhere and made it easier to carry the backpack. My two companions and I were chatting; then I left them and continued on my own at a faster pace.

The path then descended and crossed a river, only to climb steeply again into another rocky, muddy mountain path. It was winding its way again into the mountain forest that, according to history, is the road where Roland passed. It led down into the village of Zubiri, crossing a beautiful, ancient bridge. There I found an albergue and got a bed in a room with seven men; I do not know where the women were. The room was tiny, but I slept very well with all my companions, some of whom I would hike with on and off for the next few weeks. One of the pilgrims was a cop from New York City, and he had at least thirty cigars with him, one for each day on the path. They were big fat cigars from Havana, which all the men envied. We nicknamed him Smoking Bill. There was a pair of lovers from Texas and California—a beautiful woman who looked like a Mexican and a blue-eyed Texan.

The town was full of geraniums on the windows and gardens behind stone walls and a few barking guard dogs. At the entrance of the hostels, one could see the mud being washed from many shoes as pilgrims tended their aching feet and shoulders. Everyone was excited again to be walking and happy to be there. Again we all shared biographies, some complaining of divorced wives, others falling in love with new friends. It is all compressed here; you get to know others very fast when you spend all day walking and passing one another, sleeping in adjacent bunk beds, and waiting for a shower in the communal bathroom. The veil comes off very quickly, and you are who you are. You get up in the morning with little time to comb your hair or brush your teeth. One sees no lipstick, no perfume, no jewelry—just you and your companions. It is a lesson in living with oneself, and it seemed everyone had a lot of experience and had no problem.

When I walked the next day, my pack felt lighter and I walked faster. Around one in the afternoon, I had gained a certain rhythm and there was no more pain on my back or shoulders or feet—just me walking. I was concentrating on giving thanks to everything. My legs were transporting me and nature and everything; I felt part of it all with no pain. Then I concentrated on my nephews, who have a hard life, and perhaps I could help them by thinking of their angels. Then my thought went to Georg Kühlewind, a dear teacher who had just passed away in January 2006; perhaps he could accompany me on this walk whenever I thought about how much he had given to all of his students.

Here I am reminded of a passage in his article "Thinking of the Heart," which is what I am trying to practice here on the path:

> The spiritual schooling of concentration, meditation, the exercises which we perform, remain mere maneuvering motions of the ego in the interest of its own existence and strengthening, as long as man does not know the fundamental gesture of humility. Until then, the exercising is the ego's preparation for the gesture of self-humbling. But if this gesture, which justifies and sanctifies the exercising does not occur, it—the process of exercise—remains egotistical. The gesture of humility is the gesture of releasing one's self, of letting oneself fall—a paradoxical gesture, whose power consists of relinquishing the power of the ego so that the existence of the ego is destroyed in the interest of the True being which is unimaginable, neither to be fathomed nor thought up.

> As long as I am in the "right," as long as I hate, as long as I have fear, as long as I live in anxiety, as long as I wait for the other person to begin—just so long can there be no love in me. Love—even if

it be only for a single person—drives out all hate, all aversion, every fear. Whenever hate or aversion is in me, or lasting, cultivated anger, my love is of the same substance, is on the same level.

So, too, with my meditation; light maintains the life of the plant, but the plant brings with it the impurities of the soil.

When I discover: I am *never* right, I should at least draw the only logical conclusion from this view; if the other is in error, makes a mistake, then he is definitely weaker, the more besieged, the more tempted; I on the other hand, am the stronger, the healthier one. The potential for helping him is, therefore, mine, and I must initiate the first step. If I wait for him to take the first step, I declare him to be stronger; I acknowledge that he is in the right. I, however, am caught up in the error.[1]

I had decided to leave Zubiri early, by seven o'clock, and had breakfast in the next town of Larrasoaña. It was not a spectacular walk but an industrial area. Nevertheless, there were some lovely towns and places along the way. I got lost trying to find a place for breakfast and eventually found a little town with fresh bread hanging at the doors of the inhabitants. What a lovely way to start the day—with fresh bread. North Americans could learn something from old Europe about enjoying a certain quality of life. On the Camino, everyone has taken at least five weeks to enjoy the pilgrimage. That

---

1 Georg Kühlewind, *Thinking of the Heart*, Fair Oaks, CA: Rudolf Steiner College, 1987, p. 9.

*Early morning bread hanging on doors
in a small town before reaching Pamplona*

act of taking time to enjoy the days, step-by-step, sends
wonderful energy into the world. We all walk in peace
regardless of age, sex, or class, and it is a great gift to
the world.

We all begin the day with a fresh slate, not knowing
where we will sleep that night or whom or what we will
encounter; it is all blank. Nothing is planned, though we

know that the path is going in a certain direction toward one town or the other. Every step is new, and if we want to enjoy them we must remain in the present moment.

Steiner tells us, "We must each become an empty nothingness; then we can be free."[1] And in *Friend of My Heart,* Claire Blatchford writes:

> Your emptiness is your treasure.
> Don't think, "Ah! That's a paradox!"
> Go into this thought.
> Explore it, become familiar with it in every way.
> To the degree that you can empty yourself and
>   hold yourself open,
> expectant, and glad, you will be filled.
> Pay no attention to the negative thoughts that
>   try to crowd in.
> Tell them to leave.
> You will be given to the degree that you ask and
>   wait
> Just remember that the process, the opening of
>   yourself,
> is far more important than the product.
> To the degree that you are open to the hunger of
>   your times
> you will be given.
> You need not fear anything so long as you are
>   open and asking.[2]

1. Rudolf Steiner, *The Driving Force of Spiritual Powers in World History,* Toronto: Steiner Book Centre, 1972, p. 77.

2. Claire Blatchford, *Friend of My Heart: Meeting Christ in Everyday Life,* Great Barrington, MA: Lindisfarne Books, 1999, p. 158.

As I walked alone, a man walking ahead of me had a large, ugly tattoo on his calf. The man was young and Spanish with a sad, perplexing aura. I had seen him occasionally, and seeing such an ugly image, I responded with anxious feelings—here goes the self-control. I told myself to end this now. When he stopped for a drink, I walked up to him and asked him where he was from and the meaning of his tattoo. He told me that it had been a foolishness of youth, after which I continued on my way, having rid myself of wild imaginations. I was to see him several times in the next five weeks.

Rudolf Steiner speaks of such experiences:

> Just think how far human beings are from being able to think with exactitude as regards reality! Only let something stir in your soul and you will see what feelings, living hidden and unconscious in your soul, you allow to rise up. It is extremely difficult to confine oneself solely to what one has seen. Read a description of something and then ask: is the writer merely describing what he saw or is he not also calling up hundreds and hundreds of prejudices, both in feeling and in thinking, which are bound up with it? Only if you are capable of restricting yourself solely to what you have seen will you be in a position gradually to attain to thinking with exactitude.... In most cases, people have no interest in thinking with exactitude; they prefer to think in a way in which

they can enjoy the thought and feel comfortable with it.[1]

On the path I passed Smoking Bill very quickly, because the whole path was scented with his Havanas. Around two o'clock in the afternoon, I approached the famous city of Pamplona, where I walked with an older French man. I had seen him from a distance hiking with a very firm step and wearing kaki shorts. We shared some lunch and decided to take the bus when we neared the city to avoid competing with the large trucks on the road. We caught a bus and, after we got off, a Spanish couple bought us a coffee. They appreciated our pilgrimage and wished to share in it somehow.

We found our way to the center of the city, home of the famous Pamplona Bull Running. It is a beautiful, large old city, and the albergue is large like a hospital with bed-filled rooms. There I met up with some other pilgrims, one of whom was from the back woods of Maine. He had put a huge stone in my backpack as a joke and let me walk most of the day with the added weight. I decided to take his Compostela passport as a joke and returned it to him that evening.

I lingered on the large square, where all the Sunday walkers were having fun in their best attire, sipping drinks at the cafés lining the walls of the square. We did a lot of people-watching, a wonderful pastime that is rarely done where I live in the Midwest.

François, the French man, is a former military parachutist. I found it amazing that he carried at least two

---

1. Rudolf Steiner, *Old and New Methods of Initiation*, London: Rudolf Steiner Press, 1991, pp. 78–79.

*French parachutist ("Green Beret") and me
in the village of Zariquiegui, just past Pamplona*

pounds of medicine to keep him going, yet still walks faster than I do. He suffers from diabetes and many other problems, but one would never know it watching him walk the path. Never complaining, he just enjoys life after recuperating from prostrate cancer. I laughed a lot at his great humor and jokes, having fun speaking French, which I rarely do in the U.S.

In the morning, we left Pamplona with the bus number fifteen, avoiding the busy, dusty, streets, ending up on the outskirts of the city to begin our walk toward the town of Cizur Menor. I did not sleep well the previous night. People were snoring, including François, so no one slept well in the small room. We had a great breakfast of potatoes, eggs, and ham with tea and a pastry at a tiny café in the old city. On such a trip, one never knows when to expect the next real meal. I mailed more stuff to Santiago *poste restante* to avoid carrying it. My backpack continued to become lighter, leaving very few things to wear. I would wear one and wash the other.

After walking for thirty minutes, we could see the city receding and the beginning of beautiful, undulating fields of mustard green. The landscape was indigo, soft green, lemon yellow, and earthly brown—a dream for a painter or photographer. He was walking ahead, and a pilgrim returning from Santiago passed me. She had the much worn face of an older woman who had experienced many days on the road—tanned by the sun, wind, rain, heat, cold. She had walked from Switzerland and had a dog with her. She had slept out under the stars, because being gone for such a long time left little money for a place to stay. Her weathered face told many stories; her clothes were not blue jeans, but the sort of homemade woolen long skirt and jacket that I had seen much. She fell somewhere between a tramp and a pilgrim. I was a nothing pilgrim compared to this woman. She exuded an uncanny but good power that was clearly gained from much reflection and time spent alone on the path. It seemed that her companions were not the visible kind. To me, she was as close as one comes to finding the spirit of the real pilgrim of the Middle Ages. By the time she returned home, she would have walked close to two thousand miles in this pilgrimage. I felt very humble about my little walk. I wished her good luck and we parted.

We could see gigantic windmills on top of the distant mountain ridge toward which we were heading. The path was a bit muddy, but it became rocky once we reached the top. I flew down the path, and an hour later I was sitting at a table having a great lunch while waiting for François, who was having a hard time. On the other side of the ridge, the plant life was becoming Mediterranean—a lot of flowering thyme, a yellow bush tree, flowering sage, and lovely poppies starting to show up. François finally arrived in this village of Uterga, and later we continued for the next eleven kilometers.

We arrived in Puente la Reina later in the afternoon around five and walked through the old town. It is a lovely city, full of young families with children. Thanks to the influx of pilgrims, the town looks wealthy. Beginning to have an aching back, I decide to stop for a bit. I saw great colors, but not so many animals now. There were more wheat, asparagus, and other well-tended fields.

I walked alone to the next town, Mañeru. The path was not as well marked, and I got lost a couple of times. Following some elderly Germans I found the path again. I met a young Italian woman, with whom I walked off and on for the remainder of the journey. A redhead in her late twenties with a big wooden staff, she had a warm smile and appeared to be an artist.

I stopped in a beautiful old village called Cirauqui. Located on top of a hill, I found small, winding cobblestone paths that led to a café, where I had coffee and chocolate and listened to classical music. I noticed a German man was sitting quietly and thought of offering him some chocolate, and I spoke with a couple from Sweden with whom I had walked. When I left, I took the wrong path, which went through cow fields, until a bus driver gave me directions. I met the German again, and we started to talk and walk together on a path through cultivated fields. He told me that he would be staying in the town we had reached, so I said goodbye and continued on to the next town. A little later, after taking care of urgent business in the bushes, I saw the German again. His accommodations were closed so I suggested he come to the pilgrims' hostel.

We chatted and arrived in Estella o Lizarra, or "ash tree" in Basque. The comfortable hostel looked like a little monastery with its artwork and sculptures. I went into the shower and found myself having to undress in a communal bathroom next to the German—a wonderful way to get acquainted. I had not realized that I was such a prude. Instead of sleeping in the larger room, we ended up sleeping in bunk beds in a corridor by the stairs; it was more peaceful with no snoring.

After being on the Camino for more than a week, I felt myself becoming lighter. I began to laugh about everything, especially the night noises of snoring en masse. Sometimes more than fifty people in a single room, with various levels of snoring; one can become giddy. Meditation goes out the window. Where is the balance? Or is it a matter of regaining balance after being out of balance. Sharing the path with others 24/7 makes people become close very quickly.

> Now we will look at the background that helps us to understand what happened when a person became a pilgrim at that time. Today, we think abstractly that a person would undertake this to receive absolution or a blessing, to save his soul by making a pilgrimage to holy relics. This is not the case. Being a pilgrim was a way of life.

A person became a pilgrim in the same way that he became a monk by entering in a monastery. It was a complete separation from home and family, from everything; the likelihood of returning was perhaps one in two. Of every two pilgrims who went to Compostela, one returned! It is a known fact that hundreds of thousands of dead lie along these pilgrimage paths from Europe to Compostela.

The way of life at that time was strongly permeated by a completely different relationship to nature. Into the thirteenth century, people experienced nature as part of their own being. When a person moved through nature, he was moving through his own soul. Thus, those people who traveled the pilgrimage path felt less intensely, but nevertheless deeply, what Parzival had experienced as he went the path of nature initiation. Outwardly, there were certainly dangers of death, the strains of a passage from central or northern Germany to Compostela that took perhaps a year and a half. But people were not afraid of this mortal danger, because anyone who died on the pilgrim path was saved. People thought; what good does my body do me if my soul is lost? That was still strong in their consciousness. A completely different relationship to the spiritual world existed than we can imagine today. Thus, external mortality was not the frightening thing on a pilgrimage. Much more important was the fact that many sorts of inner trials took place. A mortal danger for the soul was present when the pilgrim met these various trials and temptation along the way—because in leaving home, he had separated himself from its supporting forces. When a person lived in such a small medieval city or village community, its social life supported and carried him. Desires, drives, passions were suppressed by the regular church life, the festivals, the socializing. On the road, he tore himself loose from all of this; he was free as a bird. Now all the previously repressed desires, drives, and passions rose up in him, and he had to struggle against them. We see this struggle depicted in the capitals of hundreds of columns found in places from Vézelay to Compostela. In these capitals, clairvoyant artists captured what the souls were undergoing. Art historians speak of demons or other kinds of figures they cannot explain.[1]

❧

Basically, I am having a good time, forgetting family, country, farm, children, goals, and knowledge; nothing remains, and perhaps that is what emptiness means. I am walking everyday and I am having a great time with whomever I meet. Every day that passes makes the previous one pale in comparison. The beauty of this part of Spain is beyond my imagination. I walk all day, traversing hills on red-earth paths. It is red wine country, so there are many vineyards on the southern

1. Manfred Schmidt-Brabant and Virginia Sease, *Paths of the Christian Mysteries: From Compostela to the New World,* London: Temple Lodge, 2003, pp. 86–88.

hillsides—and wine is plentiful at dinnertime, too. It is all further enlivened by majestic, gnarly old olive trees, thyme, rosemary, and fresh crimson poppies. On the hillsides and on low mountaintops, one sees small white villages shining under the warm rays of the sun, with churches standing tall and dominating the scene from afar. It is all very splendid beyond description. The only sad fact is that most of the churches are closed. In the midday heat, it would have been nice to rest and meditate within such cool beauty, but they are always closed. Pilgrims could put a little life into these old churches and chapels, but are unable to do so.

Part of my freedom is the ability to just take off and live in many places, observing as objectively as possible the pulse of a certain part of the world. I had done that all over the world, but this trip was more about me and about learning to cope with the changes in my personal life. Whereas I had paid much attention to children, husband, and all that goes with that life, yet I had left the love behind in favor of responsibility—not that I stopped loving them. Surrounded by all these pilgrims, I thoroughly enjoyed their company, waking up in the morning in the huge, busy dorms, and all the noise of starting the day on the road with all of one's belongs in a backpack.

That day we started with delicious coffee and bread. We walked through scenes of shepherds bringing their flocks to higher ground with the help of their loyal companions, the dogs. With views of soft hills in the distance, much of the path was lined and scented by pink blooming heather. We passed many abandoned *iglesia,* or chapels. I began to wonder if the Camino Santiago de Compostela is the Marian way—the way of the Virgin

Villamayor de Monjardín with castillo in the background

or the way of suffering. There are many Santa Maria's churches, cathedrals, and statues everywhere we go.

> Throughout the Middle Ages there was a sublime preparation for spiritually engendering the opposite sex within men. Man developed in himself, by concentrating, at first as a thought, what had to become a reality in him later on. Therefore, as a preparation for this, the Cult of Mary resulted in the Middle Ages. This is nothing else than concentrating to engender the female in the male, while for the female the Cult of Jesus served the parallel purpose. The Cult of Mary had its origin in this foundation.[1]

1. Rudolf Steiner, *The Temple Legend: Freemasonry and Related Occult Movements*, London: Rudolf Steiner Press, 1998, pp. 224–225.

We arrived in Santo Domingo de Calzada and stayed in an old building just for pilgrims. We were under a roof, but quite cold. The town has a special atmosphere, partaking of its illustrious past and its reawakening, thanks to the thousands of pilgrims who pass through during the summer months.

There are some stories about this mysterious place. Where was Munsalväsche, the Mystery place of the Grail founded by Titurel?[1] Where was the Grail castle? There is an extensive body of literature about this. We agree with Rudolf Steiner, who stresses throughout all his works, from his early years through the last year of his life, that the Grail was in "northern Spain." I will cite two passages that also draw our attention to specific aspects of this.

It is no accident that the Grail was to be found in Spain, where one had to go virtually miles away from what earthly reality offered, where one had to break through horny hedges in order to penetrate to the spiritual temple that enclosed the Grail.

What is described here is not meant in a merely external sense, but in a much more internal sense as well.

Rudolf Steiner draws attention to the fact that it was a very, very, hidden place in Spain. The Grail

1. The Grail castle is identified as "Munsalväsche." in Wolfram von Eschenbach's *Parzival* (c.1200), and as "Corbenic" in Thomas Malory's *Le Morte d'Arthur* (1485).

was not to be found externally among the people. "The invisible church, the supersensible church, which nevertheless can be found on the earth—it was this that concealed itself in the Mystery of the Grail."

Naturally, materialist fantasy—especially during the last centuries—always imagined the Grail castle to be like Neuschwanstein or similar castles. It was not like that! It was an earthly place, but those who did not seek the Grail passed it by. It was something that existed on the earth, but was invisible to those who did not open their eyes to it.

I have spoken about the fact that Rudolf Steiner once gave very precise indications about the location of the Grail castle.... He said—and this is already decisive—the first two Grail castles lay in the mountains called the Sierra de la Demanda. These are the mountains through which the pilgrims' path, the Camino, passes to the north; the pilgrimage site, Santo Domingo de la Calzada, lies at the only entrance to this mountain range. These were the first two sites—for we will speak of the fact that the Grail changes location.

When did the two Grail castles appear? ... Rudolf Steiner said ... it was around the turn of the eighth to the ninth centuries. These Grail events begin around the year 800. In his book *World History in the Light of the Holy Grail,* based on the descriptions of the star constellations, Walter

Johannes Stein calculated that Parzival's visit to the Grail castle could have taken place around 823, and that the other events described took place before that. This was around the time that the grave of James the apostle was discovered (815) in Compostela, and when the Camino opens itself to Europe.[1]

●

The cathedral in Santo Domingo de Calzada is superb, a glorious house of worship that has welcomed numerous pilgrims over hundreds of years. Many impressions passed through me as I stayed in the church—mostly how these people lived with an artistic quality; every fiber of their being must have been enveloped in a sacred artistic life. I can't imagine the life of the town then. Transporting the huge rocks to build all these cathedrals must have required hundreds of workers. Today, the sun shines on the cathedrals and it is very quiet, especially around noon. Pilgrims walk by and somehow resurrect these sleepy *iglesias,* or what used to live in them. The pilgrims carry in their hearts what was expressed in stones, paintings, sculptures, and poems.

Outwardly, we create messes in the world, but inwardly perhaps we are creating the beauty of the future through our intense search for answers. People are going to retreats and engaging in various spiritual activities to find meaning. As the pilgrims walk the

1. Manfred Schmidt-Brabant and Virginia Sease, *Paths of the Christian Mysteries: From Compostela to the New World,* London: Temple Lodge, 2003, lecture 4.

Afternoon stop in the state of La Rioja

path, we are seldom able to sit in these sacred places because they are closed. We are forced to sit outside on a bench, on the grass, or at a bar to meditate on life and its meaning. The church literally has closed its doors to the hundreds of pilgrims who walk this path, saying, in effect, that we should fend for ourselves, that thay are no longer there for us; that we should forget the great churches, find our own salvation. The big doors are locked; the churches are empty of believers, but the believers come with their questions and look for answers. They walk by the thousands and the numbers increase every year. They come from the four corners of the world regardless of race or religions.

That night in the auberge, after eating dinner and celebrating with endless bottles of wine, people eventually went to bed. That is when it started; everyone was snoring and I could not sleep, so I got up and went to the small dining area, where there were perhaps five people. We all started to laugh uncontrollably. A Mexican doctor acted as a symphony maestro with an invisible baton, working the snoring instruments. We laughed for at least two hours, so much so that we woke a few of the snoring members of our symphony. They were upset that we were making so much noise, and we laughed even more. A German was complaining that it was too cold, but he would not consider adding a couple of sweaters.

With each day on the path, it seems that I shed some of my past, layers of a kind of death of soul drop off my shoulders—the drain of years of motherhood, wife-hood, and all sorts of hoods are falling off. I feel lighter. I am falling in love with the word *love* itself. We are all living in a fellowship of the Camino, and sexuality finds no place except in jokes. Sometimes couples disappear to sleep in a bed and breakfast for a change, and then we see them again piled up in the dorms like the rest of us.

Every day starts anew, without any "baggage"; we have left it at home. Doctors, lawyers, hairdressers, police officers, housekeepers, teachers, poets, business people—have all left the big intellect behind and are living in the moment. Everyone feels more alive; we all get back to our "good" instincts. We are all free to be with and enjoy one another; it is an exhilarating mood for all. It is admirable to see that there are still people who put aside their whole life just to walk for days on end, being happy with the simplest of foods and putting one foot ahead of the other. For some it means awful looking toes and feet, black-bruised toes with nails coming off, tendonitis, knee or hip problems, or back pain. Not withstanding sleeping with thirty or more other souls in a room, one never hears of hard feelings or anger. We are all living for the moment, or rather in the moment. The pains that invariably come are part of the Camino, part of getting back to our original state.

Rudolf Steiner talks about it in this way:

> We need intellect and understanding so that we may find freedom, but they drive away the certainty of our instincts. A friend of mine was quite a nice person when we were young. Later in life he invited me to visit him. I had never partaken of a midday meal with scales and weights on the table. My friend first weighed everything he ate! By his intellect he had discovered how much he needed in order to maintain his body, and this exact amount was what he ate. Intellect drives out the instincts in small things, but also on a larger scale. Now it is necessary for us to find our way back to them. A sure sense for life, a firm sense in life, is needed once more. This is found by seeking our eternal element within the temporal sphere; we need to understand how the eternal finds its place in the temporal. This is what our contemporary civilization needs.[1]

Somehow, by walking all day we get in touch with the eternal within us, the element within that does not die. To do this, however, means pain. In French, the expression for someone who has studied too much is

---

1. Rudolf Steiner, *Old and New Methods of Initiation,* London: Rudolf Steiner Press, 1991, p. 43.

grosse tête. These big heads have lost their common sense, and having a big head here can get one into plenty of trouble, such as getting lost by being unable to trust one's instincts.

The next morning, the German had caught a cold and was not feeling too well. After a few miles, in the town of Gragnon, he decided to stop and take the bus to the next village because he had a fever. I went on, hating to leave a sick friend. My maternal instinct had to be left behind—I am not a mother here but a pilgrim. I walked for the rest of the day singing whatever came to my mind, but invariably the same melody. Singing and walking, it seems, go together. I saw others, too, who would be singing out songs, but becoming quiet as we passed one another. Many retired French couples were walking.

I arrived in the next town, Beldorado, and stayed in a lovely little hostel with my companions. This town was a delightful place, with a large square with several sidewalk cafés where one could sit and soak up the last rays of the sun. The innkeeper seemed serious about his job as a protector of pilgrims. He had on a black outfit with a big cross hanging from his neck, attempting it seems to drive out all our demons. Wonderful music was playing.

I took a shower and went for a walk in town, where I bumped into the German who had gotten a room to fend off his cold. We were going to have supper together, but halfway through the meal I said, "You do not have to be polite; you should go to bed and get some rest." He went and I lost track of him for several days.

I love walking all day and feel increasingly rejuvenated through the simple freedom of enjoying everyone. For me, this gift of walking allows life and recovers my true nature; the people we encounter help us in this. My heart seems to open more and more to everything—nature, man, woman, whatever. What is nice is to be able to look into other's eyes and truly see them and perhaps truly be seen. Since we have nothing to do all day but look at everything, it is great to look at one another and truly see who stands before us while listening to what they have to say. It is rare to encounter a pilgrim who does not listen. A few keep to themselves, and we honor their need for solitude. We are together and for one another on the path. I am reminded of Christoher Bamford's words on companions:

> Here we may note briefly how extraordinary in the Christian tradition this idea of a double monastery is. Indeed, while the rest of Christendom seemed to flee the reality of the sexes in terror and rage, fear and trembling, for the Celtic tradition the idea of men and women—of human beings—working together spiritually was the most natural thing. Besides the double monasteries, there are two other Celtic institutions that speak of this deep sense of the transgenderal recognition of individuality and community as two sides of one coin. There is the institution of *conhospitae,* or women taking active part in monastic worship, helping celebrate the Mass, carrying the wine. Then there is the tradition of "soul friends"—*anamchara*—wherein two pilgrims of

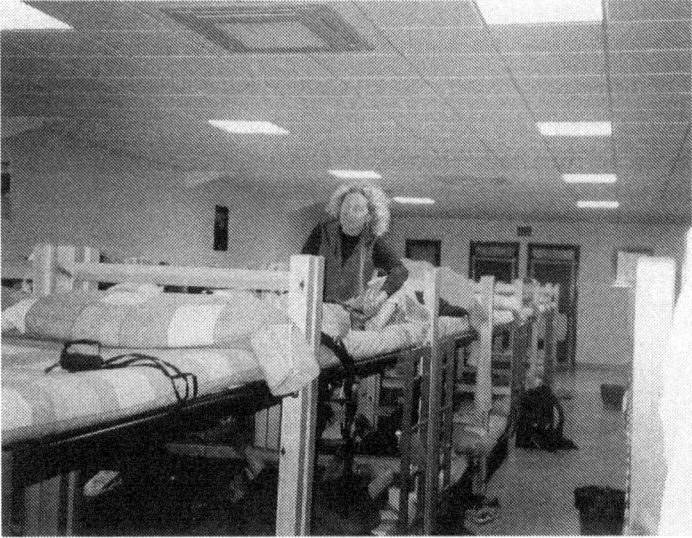

On the way to Burgos—a typical shared lodging

the way act as spiritual friends or counselors to
each other in a relation of mutuality, intimacy,
confidence, and selfless love. Already in Druid
times, it was said in Ireland that "anyone without a soul friend is like a soul without a body."
And later, in Christian times, this tradition—
which often joined the sexes, so that a man and a
woman, a monk and a nun, would be soul friends
to each other—gave rise to a deep practice of
intimate, private confession, of repeated forgive-
ness of sins. And this then spread across Europe,
where the tradition of confession was still at that
time public. Implicit, too, in the *anamchara,* or
"soul friend," tradition is the belief that a complete human being is constituted of the mysti-

cal marriage of male and female, a union and a friendship that is both psychological and actual, inner and outer. The essence here is "hospitality"—hospitality as *compassion in action*. In a way, the Celtic tradition is the path of hospitality: of openness to the beings of heaven, Earth, and the middle realms. Put another way, it is the path of making a safe place, a transforming hearth, for the divine, the cosmic, the elemental, and the human—above all, the human. Wherever the Celtic saints went in their wanderings, their first act was to provide shelter, hospice, medicine, and fellowship—the only solid foundation for any true culture or spirituality.[1]

Doesn't this also describe the Camino?

I went on the next day through more enchanting scenery, woods, and mountains. I had lunch in an unappetizing village, Villafranca Montes de Oca. The path then began to climb into oak and pine forests and was deserted. It did not have the good feeling I experienced in other places, so perhaps this was a kind of robbers' nest and difficult in the Middle Ages. I passed several other woman hikers and had a chat and snack in a pine forest by the side of the path. I had passed the young German woman many times before, and she

1. Christopher Bamford, *The Voice of the Eagle: The Heart of Celtic Christianity,* Great Barrington, MA: Lindisfarne Books, 2000, p. 36.

was always stopping in magical places and enjoying the peace. Here the air had the sweet smell of pine needles.

John Brierley in his *Pilgrim's Guide to the Camino de Santiago* says, "The village of Villafranca is located at the foot of the Montes de Ocas, formerly a wild unpopulated area and notorious for the bandits that roamed its slopes preying on pilgrims. The bandits in turn would doubtless pray for protection from the Saint himself in the safety of the Church of Santiago."[1] In this walk one can always sense the past, and one could feel this certain uneasiness while walking there. Fear was still there, and one had to work to dissipate this unhealthy aura by looking and concentrating on the lovely scenery, flowers, plant life.

I arrived in San Juan de Ortega, a small, isolated, town and a great little oasis; I stayed with two Swedish sisters, who were trying to help a Mexican addict. We did not know how he would make it to the end, given the way he was drinking beer, smoking grass, and using whatever else was at his disposal. Perhaps the path would help him. It was nice to see the two young women trying to put some sense into this man with a lost soul. In the evening we were serenaded by a modern troubadour who carried his accordion with him through the Camino and sang for everyone. He had come from New Zealand via South America and sang beautiful songs of freedom.

---

1. John Brierley, *A Pilgrim's Guide to the Camino de Santiago: The Ancient Pilgrim Path also Known as Camino Francés: The Way of St. James from St. Jean Pied de Port to Santiago de Compostela,* Forres, Scotland: Findhorn Press, 2006, p. 133.

Walking alone again, I missed the friends I had been walking with. Here the lesson must be to enjoy whoever you encounter today, because you might never meet again in this lifetime.

I took the bus into Burgos after walking to the edge of that big city with two Austrian women (mother and daughter) of Eastern origin.

I do not enjoy walking on city streets and crossing large roads while fending off traffic and the smell of bad air. We all waited for the bus, chatted, and shared experiences, while the hardcore pilgrims, who had made a vow not to take any public transportation, continued with very determined and heroic steps. Our hearts went to them as we passed them on the bus.

We all went into the large Gothic Cathedral of Santa Maria in Burgos, a monumental structure where I spent quite a long time admiring the stained-glass windows and overall beauty.

> Those who built the great cathedrals of medieval times were the great Freemasons. They were aware of the importance of the fact that what was spoken by the priest should be reflected back from the individual walls and the whole congregation immersed in a sea of sound, breathing and fluctuating in significant vibration which would exercise still greater effect on the astral body than on the physical ear.[1]

I sat in the square and watched the tourists and pilgrims while eating lunch and figuring out where I

1. Rudolf Steiner, *The Temple Legend: Freemasonry and Related Occult Movements,* London: Rudolf Steiner Press, 1998, p. 86.

Burgos Cathedral

would spend the night. I saw one of the pilgrims from Brazil, who was sweating profusely; he had not taken the bus into the city, and I told him to have a rest and a drink. Then we chatted and I wanted to know the time. I told him I had lost my watch in the last few days. Listening, he proceeded to take a blue watch out of his pockets. My watch! He had found it on the path. I told him thank you, and he went on his way to the hostel. Outside, on the big square by the Cathedral, many pilgrims were resting tired feet and enjoying a sunny afternoon. Monks with beautiful designer clothes and shiny black boots were walking around looking like they had arrived from the Vatican. Very impressive, but I ask myself: Who are the real monks here?

In the church I had met a woman doctor from Budapest, and we decided to take a city bus to the pilgrims' hostel a few miles on the other side of the city. The place was a zoo. There were at least 150 people in a small long building with no visible windows and sleeping on top of one another. I could not imagine staying there. I shared a light supper of fresh strawberries, yogurt, cheese, bread, and juice, speaking Spanish with a Mexican doctor and two older men from Spain.

Later, I looked at my friend from Budapest who speaks absolutely no English or French or Spanish, but only Hungarian. In her hilarious, newfound language, she said, "Me no like here, less go." I acquiesced happily, and we took a taxi that dropped us in the next town, thus avoiding all the traffic and commotion of a large city. When we arrived we laughed a lot at our unpilgrim-like way. We slept in a small hostel, where the young couple from Texas and California stayed as well. The evening was not without some minor happenings. The bathroom was fully flooded and my friend wanted to clean it up, but I did not. We did not have enough towels for all the water. In any case, we went off to bed happy to be away from those cramped quarters. Pilgrims do not have to be treated in this way in a huge city, but we should just be thankful that there was a place to stay.

In the next few days we will start walking on the long, hot *meseta* (the high plateau of central Spain);

Lunch break in Burgos

many are taking a bus to avoid this dreaded and, for some, boring part of the road. I love it all— I walk flat land, mountains, hills, forests, and whatever the terrain there is.

These words from Rudolf Steiner remind me of our task.

In very ancient times, people saw life in every cloud formation, every flash of lightening, every roll of thunder, in every living plant, and so on. In a sense, they breathed in life and thus understood it, and without any effort they were in the midst of life. They only had to take in life from the outside. In contrast, in our evolutionary stage our concepts can grasp only what is dead, and the outer environment can no longer give us what is alive. Therefore, we must bring forth this living element out of the inner most core of our being.

It is not enough to understand history merely theoretically, with our intellect, for then history appears much too uniform and unvarying. We have to put ourselves with all our soul into the way people in past epochs experienced history....

We modern people can no longer feel the divine element within us, as ancient people still could, we must work to reach the divine realm.... The condition of our soul will change only when our spiritual understanding of our place in nature becomes inwardly alive.

It can change only when the same feeling, perception, and soul conditions that live in love also accompany the act of knowing. When we permeate our knowledge with the experience of love, then our knowledge can approach the Mystery of Golgotha.[1]

In normal life, love is bound to the human instincts, to the life of desires, but it is possible to extricate love out of normal life in the same way as the faculty of memory. The power

---

1. Rudolf Steiner, *Earthly Knowledge and Heavenly Wisdom*, Hudson, NY: Anthroposophic Press, 1991, pp. 124ff.

of love can be developed, if by means of it we are able to obtain real objectivity. Whereas in normal life the original impetus for love comes from within the human being, it is also possible to develop this love through being immersed in outer objects so that we are able to forget ourselves and become one with the outer objects. If we perform an action in such a way that it does not arise out of our inner impulses which originate in our desires and instincts, but out of love for what is around us, then we have the kind of love which is at the same time the power of human freedom.[1]

✺

We started the next day refreshed, ready for another beautiful sunny day; rain would have been another story. I stopped for breakfast in the town of Rabé de las Calzados and lost my Hungarian friend in the winding streets of this little town from the Middle Ages. I stopped and enjoyed the usual tea or coffee with bread and jams. All sorts of foreigners end up in little towns like this, and the owner of this café was French. She had settled in Rabé de las Calzados to take care of the pilgrims in lovely renovated stone homes. The path continued between stone walls, and I met a woman from Nova Scotia resting on a stone wall. I continued on at my new, faster pace.

1. Rudolf Steiner, *Spiritual Research: Methods and Results,* Blauvelt, NY: Garber, 1981, pp. 221–222.

The scenery became increasingly beautiful, with spectacular little white villages shining on top of hills. We were on a *meseta* at about 2800 feet, and one wants to stop in all the villages. Lunch breaks are especially enjoyable, because many of us invariably enter one of the villages to sit at a café for a treat—for both the stomach and the eyes. We sit on the stairs of a chapel or on the roadside while sipping delicious drinks; or we bathe our tired feet in ancient fountains shaped like shells, mythical beings, or a lion's head with water spurting from the mouth.

For the German and Nordic pilgrims, after 12:00 means it's finally time to have a glass of beer. For the others it is coffee. We chat with new friends, see new faces, and old friends ask about the ones we haven't seen for a while.

I arrived in the little town of Hontanas, which is well hidden and cannot be seen until it is suddenly there. It appears where three hills meet. One descends from the *meseta* and finds it at the bottom, well built and away from casual eyes. It was still early, so I decided to continue on to the next town, another seven to nine kilometers farther. I stayed for lunch, however, along with about thirty others. The square is next to the somber old church of the Assumption. We were all resting and drinking from the great fountain and enjoying this typical pilgrims' village under the protective eyes of the simple church. There were many Germans in Hontanas who had paid quite a bit of money to an organized tour company to walk the Camino in style—traveling with their big Mercedes trucks and a kind of wagon filled with their stuff. It

Before Hontanas—the doctor from Budapest

met them at lunch and in the evening, so they did not need to carry anything. It was hot, and the rest of us were sweating it out.

My Hungarian friend arrived in the village just as I was moving on. We said we would catch up later. After a couple of hours of walking among more enchanting scenery filled with ancient ruins, I passed a very old monastery in ruins. This was a special spot, so I sat by the side of the deserted road for a long time, trying to make history come alive in this beautiful area of northern Spain. According to *A Pilgrims' Guide to the Camino de Santiago*, Arco San Antón was the ancient monastery and hospice of the Antoine Order founded in France during the eleventh century. It was connected with the work of the Egyptian desert father and hermit Saint Anthony. "The order's sacred symbol was a 'T' shaped cross known as the TAU (the nineteenth letter of the Greek alphabet). The order was known for its ability to cure the medieval scourge known as St. Anthony's fire (a kind of gangrenous skin disease) by using the power of the TAU (Love) in its healing practice" (p. 160). Rudolf Steiner speaks about it as well:

> Everything must in the end undergo a schooling. The last four hundred years were in fact a schooling for humanity—the school of godlessness, in which there was purely human experimentation, a return to chaos if seen from a particular point of view. Everyone is experimenting today, without being aware of the connection with higher worlds—apart from those who have once more sought and found that connection with the spiritual realms. Nearly everyone lives entirely for himself today without perceiving anything of the real and all-penetrating common design. That of course is the cause of the dreadful dissatisfaction everywhere.

> What we need is a renewal of the Grail Chivalry in a modern form. Anyone who can approach this will thereby come to know the real forces which today are still lying hidden in the course of human evolution.

> Today so many people take up the old symbols without understanding them.... Such understanding is to be sought in precisely those things which redeem mere natural forces; in penetrating and mastering what is living in the same way that the geometrician penetrates and masters the inani-

mate with his rule, compasses, spirit level and so forth; and in working upon the living in the same way those who build a temple put the unliving stones together. That is the great Masonic concept of the future.

There is a very ancient symbol in Freemasonry, the so-called Tau:

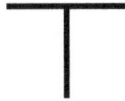

T

This Tao sign plays a major role in Freemasonry. It is basically nothing else than a Cross from which the upper arm has been taken away. The Mineral Kingdom is excluded in order to obtain the Cross at all—man already controls that. If one lets the Plant Kingdom come into play then one obtains the Cross directed upward:

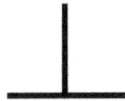

⊥

What unfolds itself from the earth, from the soul, as power over the earth, is the symbol of future Freemasonry....

The Tao sign symbolizes a totally new power, based on freedom, and consisting in the awakening of a new natural force.... What is expressed by the Tao is a driving force which can only be set in motion by the power of selfless love. It will be possible to use this power to drive machines, which will, however, cease to function if egoistical people make use of them.[1]

🐚

I finally tore myself away from this amazing place as a group of Italian bicyclists passed. I walked on, admiring the incredible views of another castle town in the distance, and finally was able to see Castrojeriz emerge on top of a high distant hill.

After a long walk of thirty-three kilometers, I arrived that evening only mildly exhausted at a sober hostel. The hostel keeper had the traditional outfit and is somewhat famous on the Camino circuit. He had a long ponytail, was dressed in black, and looked a bit foreboding. We could not make too much noise, unlike the chaotic albergues I had become used to. He was trying to maintain an aura of the serious pilgrim of the past. In any case, it was fine with me. There I met the Mexican doctor and the young redhead Italian artist; they had walked an additional eight kilometers, and they were very tired.

I went out to look at the city, which looked prosperous, with many houses appearing to be second homes. They were renovating the large sixteenth-century cathedral Iglesia de San Juan, so I was unable to go in. The town had numerous shops, and, for a relatively isolated town, it was surprisingly alive.

---

1. Rudolf Steiner, *The Temple Legend: Freemasonry and Related Occult Movements,* London: Rudolf Steiner Press, 1997, pp. 283–285.

Italian artist and the Mexican doctor on the meseta

Again I am reminded that this Camino is a Marian way. Cathedrals are everywhere. One here at the entrance of Castrojeriz is called La Colegiata de Santa María del Manzano—Mary of the Apple Tree Church; I loved that name. The Virgin Mary is everywhere; perhaps all the women are becoming virgins on this walk. As we walk we unburden ourselves of psychological weights. To spare our backs, we carry only the essentials; I think we do the same inwardly. What are the essentials we carry within? We each figure that out as we walk. How do we unburden ourselves of this extra baggage? We leave behind whatever caused anxiety, pain, or frustration, all of which is unnecessary. We keep only what is carved into our hearts, which is different for each of us. As we walk, we have to put one foot ahead of the other, going slowly so that we must

"Castle Town" in the state of Castilla y León

stay in the present and enjoy what the scenery has to offer—wind, sun, the elements, animals, nature, and friends. As we walk, we become lighter in heart and soul, and the physical weight simply disappears. As we unburden our souls of the psychological weight, we can carry the physical weight much more easily. This is the healing aspect of this Camino. We are watched over by great beings, as well as by human friends who are called to walk together for a while. It is not all chance; we meet people and know that they are not strangers.

The Camino becomes busier, and it is not even the height of summer season. These people are called in some way to make the journey and join others of like mind in the spiritual search. It reminds me of Rudolf Steiner's words:

> The human being has grown out of the group soul condition and emancipates himself from it

The Italian and the Mexican doctor—
looking back at Castrojeriz

increasingly. If we look at groups instead of the
souls, we have family connections, connections of
tribe and nation, and finally connected races. The
race corresponds to a group soul. All these group
connections of early humanity are what man out-
grows and the more we advance the more the race
conception loses its meaning.

We stand today at a transitional point; race will
gradually disappear entirely and something else
will take its place. Those who will again grasp
spiritual truth as it has been described will be
led together of their own free will. Those will the
connections of a later age. The human beings of
earlier times were born into connections, born
into tribe, race. Later we shall live in the connections and associations which men create for

themselves, uniting in groups with those of similar ideas while retaining their complete freedom
and individuality....

The individual voluntarily allow their feelings to
stream together and this again causes the form-
ing of something which goes beyond the merely
emancipated man. An emancipated human being
possesses his individual soul which is never lost
when it has once been attained. But when men
find themselves together in voluntary associations they group themselves round centers. The
feelings streaming in this way to a center once
more give beings the opportunity of working as
a kind of group souls. All the earlier group souls
were beings who made man unfree. These beings,
however are compatible with man's complete
freedom and individuality. Indeed, in a certain
respect we may say that they support their existence on human harmony; it will lie in the souls
of men themselves whether or not they give as
many as possible of such higher souls the opportunity of descending to man. The more that men
are divided the fewer lofty souls will descend into
the human sphere. The more the associations are
formed where feelings of fellowship are developed
with complete freedom, the more lofty beings will
descend and the more rapidly the earthly planet
will be spiritualized.[1]

❧

1. Rudolf Steiner, *The Influence of Spiritual Beings upon Man*, New
York, Anthroposophic Press, 1961, pp. 155–156.

We can feel the special atmosphere all around the Camino. We all receive our Camino passport, which in Saint-Jean-Pied-de-Port is administered by the Brothers of St. John as volunteers. We are all part of that fellowship as we begin our path, and spiritual beings watch over us as we travel the path as brothers and sisters. We could therefore understand the whole Milky Way mirrored on the Camino de Compostela, with wise beings watching over the path and directing from above. St. James and St. John seem to have had a massive influence from the seventh to ninth centuries in this area of Spain, continuing into later centuries. "The Santiago story reemerges in 813 when a shepherd named Pelayo was drawn to a field by a 'bright light' or star. Thus we have, the field *compos* of the stars *stella* of St. James *Sant Iago,* which gives us Santiago de Compostela."[1]

> The circumstances surrounding the discovery of the Saint's body are related in a document of the year 1100 entitled *Historia Compostela*. It recounts that in the year 815, during the reign of the Asturian king Alphonso II "The Chaste," and when Theodomirus was bishop of Iria-Flavia, a hermit named Pelayo saw some lights glimmering near his hermitage, which were also seen by some nearby peasants, according to the chronicles. The bishop was informed and came to the spot, located about twelve miles from Iria, guided by the lights. Pushing back the undergrowth with his hands, he found, "guarded by marble stones," the

1. John Brierley, *A Pilgrim's Guide to the Camino de Santiago,* Forres, Scotland: Findhorn Press, 2006, p. 37.

tomb with the remains of St. James. Shortly after this, Alfonso II had a small church built on the spot and later founded the Monastery [San Paio de] Antealtares to house the Benedictine monks who were entrusted with guarding the tomb and promoting the cult. This is the origin of Santiago de Compostela, whose name is popularly associated with the lights or star beams that showed Pelayo the way to the Saint's tomb. Alfonso ceded the three miles property around the church to the bishop Iria-Flavia (who would subsequently found the diocese of Compostela) as well as the rights over its inhabitants. Thus the great Christian story was born, a story that would attract hundreds of thousands of people to Santiago over the course of the following centuries. The creation of this tradition meant that the weakened Spanish church, plunged into division and theological controversy and hedged in by pressure from the Islamic caliphate of Cordoba, had created a powerful idea which would rescue it from isolation.[1]

Many of the associations that take care of the pilgrims are very old and are linked with various orders such as the Knights Templar and the Order of St. John, La Federación Española de Asociaciones de Amigos del Camino de Santiago, the Brothers Hospitallers of St. John of God, and The Confraternity of Saint James.

It is no less than St. James and the brotherhood of St. John of the cross. Now we have St. James cult

---

1 Maria Unceta, *La Catedral de Santiago de Compostela,* Spain: Aldeasa, 2004, p. 12.

here in Spain, and St. John having a strong influence through Scotus Erogina in the Celtic Church, his deep study of sacred Christian works (Scotus dies in 877). These influences are all intertwined...we must also remember that the western coast of Spain, Galicia was always in contact with the Celtic Mysteries through navigation and pilgrims which went on from antiquity and never stopped....

Celts had been the first Aryans to arrive in Northern Europe and they seem, at one time to have spread over most of the Continent. Later on, in historical times, they were to be found chiefly throughout that wide district—including most of modern France and a great part of Spain and Portugal.... the conflict between Celt and Teuton dragged on in Ireland until 1921.... One contingent of the old Celtic inhabitants of this island, or *Britons,* driven to the tip of Cornwall, decided to leave these shores altogether. They sailed back to the Continent, and there established themselves in the seaboard district which still bears the name of *Brittany.*[1]

We can be sure that the work of Scotus Eriugina reached these shores during that century; they also came through the Pyrenees from Scotus studies in France.[2]

---

1 Owen Barfield, *History in English Words,* Great Barrington, MA: Lindisfarne Books, 2002, p. 45.

2 It is obvious that I am not a priest or scholar, but just a pilgrim who reads a lot. For more on Scotus, read Christopher Bamford's marvelous book, *The Voice of the Eagle: The Heart of Celtic Christianity,* Great Barrington, MA: Lindisfarne Books, 2000.

Rudolf Steiner talks about John, James, and Peter:

> Now I must tell you something that is easy for a modern's intellect to follow but difficult for one's soul attitude to understand. At the dawn of Christianity a man always saw the *higher* spiritual element looking through the physical organism. He did not feel *what* we feel when we name someone—he named people *sensibly*. Supposing one called someone James. James really means water. Water is the spiritual scientific expression for the soul, so that if I call someone James I am saying that the soul element is shining through his body. Thereby I wisely give him a name that indicates he belongs to water. So if I, as an initiate give someone this name James then to me he is a symbol for water (*jam* in Hebrew). James is nothing else than the scientific name for an initiate (an enlightened, knowing person, sage) who especially controls the force of occult (hidden forces) water.

> Called by their initiation names these were the three disciples who were taken to Mt. Tabor: James means water, Peter means earth rock (*jabasha* in Hebrew), and John means air (*ruah*). So John means one who has come to his higher self. This takes you deep into esotericism. If one goes back to the earth's third root race or Lemurian epoch men only had the lower principles and they breathed through gills—they were not breathing air yet. Lungs and lung breathing only arose later. This event coincides with a fertilization by the higher self. According to the hermetic principle

air is nothing else than the lower for the upper, the higher self. If I call someone John then he is one who controls air's occult forces. So in these four names you have representatives of earth, water, air and fire. These are the names of the four who go up to Mt. Tabor. If you imagine these four together on the mountain of transfiguration than you also have the initiates who control the four elements or the lords of the four elements: fire, water, air, earth.[1]

We see that we have with the three apostles: St. Peter is the rock, St. John is the air, St. James is the water, whereas *Christ* is fire (fire is *nour* in Hebrew).

On the Camino, St. James—who was an initiate of the occult forces of water, or as Steiner says, of the soul—is our patron. Whether we believe in him or not makes no difference; he is there. His remains were discovered around 813. When this pilgrimage started around 778, Charlemagne was crossing the Pyrenees, coming to the aid of Roland and to push back the Saracens. Deeply Christian, Charlemagne was proclaimed Emperor in Rome in 800. Though he was unable to read, he had other means of gaining knowledge. He was widely admired, and many considered him an initiate king.

Scotus Eriugina was "born early in the ninth century, for by CE 850 or 851 he was already in France, a scholar of repute attached to the Cathedral School of Laon,

---

1. Rudolf Steiner, "Theosophy in Connection with the Gospel of St. John," Lecture, March 5, 1906, unpublished typescript, p. 48.

and well known to the court of King Charles the Bald."[1] John the Scot worked deeply with St. John's gospel and influenced many thinkers during the centuries that followed, with the result that the influence of St. John spread over Europe, whereas Peter established the Church in Rome. We can therefore see the enormous influence of John, Peter, and James, who stood by Christ, throughout the whole Camino.

We could also say that Peter is the earth, and the physical body; James is the etheric body, or life forces, and water; John is the astral, or feeling emotion body, and air; and Christ the fire element for our higher "I" force. This is one view, or one picture. Because St. James is an initiate of water, we could say that we walk the way of nature on this path, with a strong emphasis on the etheric body, or body of life forces. For some pilgrims, this could be an initiation into the spiritual world through the help of St. James, leading the pilgrim to experience a meeting with the Christ being in the realm of etheric forces and, in fact, to know the Christ as St. Paul did at Damascus. This might be why all these people, young and old, are flocking to this particular area of the world in unprecedented numbers. We can also say that the ether, the world of etheric, or life, forces is the realm that retains our memories. Our whole planet is undergoing drastic changes, whereby human consciousness is changing and coming into harmony with events in the world of spirit. We all go

---

1. Christopher Bamford, *The Voice of the Eagle: The Heart of Celtic Christianity,* Great Barrington, MA: Lindisfarne Books, 2000, p. 54.

to sleep to the same realm and can "catch" the same dreams. One such dream is going to Compostela.

🌸

After my walk in the castle town, Castrojeriz, and looking at the old ruins—some from the Romans and the Visigoths who lived here—I retired in the nice albergue with my friends the Italian artist and the Mexican doctor. I had a lovely supper in the bar next door with a Spanish woman walking the Camino; she was of the strong opinion that if you take any kind of transportation along the Camino you are cheating, so of course I did not say anything. I did not want her to become upset. One must have freedom to decide what one needs and not impose it on others.

The area is full of little fortified villages. They are jewel villages, invaded by very few tourists. Mostly, the only people who find their way here are the pilgrims. One can see old dilapidated castles overlooking some of the villages. This one is well maintained and beautiful. Many of the albergues do not charge money; in the tradition of the past, one pays what one can. Walking among the hills, I discovered little villages around the corner and into a small valley, hidden pearls in the countryside. There are still many cultivated fields, soft hills, old convents, and old ruins. I walked alone, singing most of the day—songs of brother wind, mother earth, and sister rain and so on, making up the melody. I came to wish that I was a better singer, because one can feel that singing belongs on this path.

Walking was great again and helped empty me. I felt the need to let go. Every single moment is an experience in letting go. Walking, we pass through enchanting sights at every corner, and we must let go of each one, because five minutes later another worthy sight will appear. Even though I go along at my own pace, three to six kilometers per hour, it is hard to give up the past. The past holds on to us, and I must learn not to *want*, but just be *with*, since nothing really belongs to us.

The next day we all started early, following the usual breakfast and storage of water for the day. We climbed into the heart of the *meseta*, long, monotonous, and flat on that plateau, 2500 to 3000 feet up, which will take us all the way to León, almost two hundred kilometers. We climbed up from Castrojeriz, and looking back we could see the fortress town in the distance, as well as some police on the path helping the *pelegrinos* with water; they would need it, because there's no water above. The beginning of the climb was a long hill leading into the *meseta*, even though we are high up already. I walked with the Mexican and the Italian artist for the day. We picked up the pace and walked quite fast while sharing our biographies. We were laughing most of the way and admiring the Mediterranean landscape that now surrounded us, with many red poppies smiling at us from their little soft heads as they straighten up to reach for the sun. The Mexican doctor had us both in stitches. He told us that, all along the road, the *coquelicots* (French for poppies) were sending us little red kisses, and that we had to love them back.

Poppies

Here again are Rudolf Steiner's words:

If you could observe the sun forces as they stream down onto the bodies of plants as they grow out of the earth—these plants with their roots and leaves ending above with blossoms enveloped by astrality into which the spiritual sun-forces pour—if you could perceive with a spiritual eye these forces which enter mysteriously through the blossom, you would "hear" them as the spiritual music of the spheres—audible, it is true, only to "spirit ears." Spiritual tones penetrate mysteriously into the flowers of plants. This is the secret of plant-growth; each individual blossom is an expression of tones that give its form and the fruit its character. The sun-tones are caught up by the plant and reign within it as spirit.

You know perhaps, how form can be created in the material world through sound. Think of [Ernst] Chladni's sound figures, how powder scattered over a plate takes on certain patterns or figures when subjected to sound; these figures are the expression of the sound that caused them. Just as physical sound is caught in this powder, the spiritual sound of the sun is captured and drawn in by flower and fruit. It is hidden mysteriously within the seed and when the new plant springs from the seed it is this trapped and absorbed sound that conjures up forth the form of the plant.

Clairvoyant consciousness surveys our surrounding world of plants and in the flowers that carpet our earth's surface it sees everywhere the reflex of the sun tones. What Goethe says is true, "The sun intones his ancient song," but it is also true that these sun tones stream down, are absorbed by the plants and re-appear when the new plant springs from the seed. For the sun tones resound in the forms of the plants, re-echoing into space the music of the spheres.[1]

---

1. Rudolf Steiner, *Universe, Earth, and Man: In Their Relationship to Egyptian Myths and Modern Civilization*, London: Rudolf Steiner Press, 1987, p. 120.

Seen from another perspective, Steiner says:

> People walk about on the earth, and it is a con-
> glomeration of rocks and stones to them, but they
> must learn to grasp that everything surrounding
> them is a true physical expression of the Spirit
> of the Earth.... The pupil must educate himself
> to see in every single flower in a meadow the
> outer expression of a living being, the expression
> of the Spirit dwelling in the earth. Every stone,
> every plant, every flower is for the pupil the outer
> expression of the indwelling Earth Spirit, its phys-
> iognomy that speaks.[1]

●

We walked on, enjoying the scene full of wheat fields,
while talking about our personal lives. Suddenly it
occurred to me to call the German, because the Italian
artist had a cell phone, and the German had given me
his address and phone numbers in case we did not meet
again. When I called, lo and behold he answered. I was
very happy to hear from him and asked where he was.
He had taken a bus and met up with smoking Bill and
was one day ahead of me. When I arrived in Fomista,
our next town, I decided to take a taxi the next day and
meet the rest of the gang at the next leg of the journey,
which was Carrión de los Condes.

The hostel was comfortable, and I paid my visit to
the church, which was very quiet and solemn; a nice

1. Rudolf Steiner, *Rosicrucian Wisdom: An Introduction,* London:
Rudolf Steiner Press, 2000, p. 162.

An old town in the state of Palencia

end to a long day. I had to skip a day here and there in order to arrive in Santiago in time for my return flight home. I might as well do it here. It says in the book that this walk is by the highway and not very enjoyable, so the next morning I got up very early. It was still dark and I took a taxi that dropped me off by a café in the town. The landscape had not yet awakened, but a few pilgrims were already walking in the cold, humid darkness. At the café, I had my breakfast and called the German and the others and told them where I was. We planned to meet on the path.

"Peacekeepers"—the German and Smoking Bill

By the time I started walking, the sun had risen on the *meseta*. This part of the *meseta* would be a very long, flat landscape, and I thought I might as well go on; they will catch up. I walked part of the way with a retired French couple from southern France. I then continued alone, expecting to see the German and Smoking Bill. By 1:30, I'd had enough after walking for seven hours, so I stopped at the first café I'd seen all day, where many other tired pilgrims were enjoying a well-deserved meal. After thirty minutes or so, the German arrived, and it was wonderful to see each other. We got caught up

Terradillos de los Templarios

about everything and everyone we knew while waiting for Smoking Bill and his new friend, a pretty German girl who was a linguist and barmaid.

Together, we continued on to the next albergue and found a pleasant hostel serving great food. There we stayed in our own room with only four beds. The dining room was quite full of pilgrims; the woman who served us was very young and had a great sense of humor. She joked with me, and after the meal gave me a big kiss—a very unusual Spaniard.

After a long day, we were finally able to sleep without a symphony of snoring. Before retiring, however,

Albergue Jacques deMolay
Terradillos de los Templarios

we all went for a walk to watch the sunset. The village is isolated and extremely poor and had an abandoned look about it. Its name, Terradillos de los Templarios, has left no trace of its former past. I tried to get into the life of the place but could not. According to the guidebook: "After the relative luxury of Carrion here in Terradillos de los Templarios we experience the simplicity of this humble village.... Formerly a stronghold of the Knights Templar, nothing on the physical level, remains of this noble Order but its spirit lives on in the place name."[1] Some of their teachings could be described in this way:

> The pupil of the Rosicrucian school had repeatedly to bring the picture before his mind of the

---

1. John Brierley, *A Pilgrim's Guide to the Camino de Santiago*, Forres, Scotland: Findhorn Press, 2006, p. 182.

plant with its head downward and the reproductive organs stretching toward the beam of the sun. The sunbeam was called the "holy lance of love" that must penetrate the plant to enable the seeds to mature and grow. The pupil was told: Contemplate man in relation to the plant; compare the substance of which man is composed with that of the plants. Man, the plant turned upside down, has permeated his substance, his flesh, with physical cravings, passion, and sensuality. The plant stretches in purity and chastity the reproductive organs toward the fertilizing sacred lance of love. This stage will be reached by an individual when he has completely purified all cravings. In the future, when earth evolution has reached its height, a person will attain this ideal. When no impure desires permeate the lower organs, a person will become as chaste and pure as the plant is now....

Thus the human being's development takes him through the kingdoms of nature. He purifies his being until he develops organs of which there are of yet only indications. The beginning of a future productive power can be seen when human beings create something that is sacred and noble—a force they will fully possess once their lower nature is purified....

Thus, what the Rosicrucian pupil depicted to himself represents on a lower level the great future ideal of humankind, attainable when the lower nature has been purified and chastely offers itself to the spiritualized sun of the future.... The Rosicrucian pupil grasped all of this in its spiritual meaning. He understood it as the mystery of the Holy Grail—humankind's highest ideal. He saw the whole of nature permeating and glowing with spiritual meaning. When everything is thus seen as symbol of the spirit, one is on the way to attain imaginative knowledge; color and sound separate from objects and become independent. Space becomes a world of color and sound in which spiritual beings announce their presence. The pupil rises from imaginative knowledge to direct knowledge of the spiritual realm. That is the path of the Rosicrucian pupil at the second stage of training.[1]

❀

I was very surprised to look at the buildings, which were very similar to the houses I had seen in Afghanistan and the Middle East, made of red mud or adobe construction. So far away, yet so similar, I had never seen such construction in France or Italy. I was happy to be with my traveling companions again. I went to sleep that night quite tired and awoke ready for the next *meseta* day.

The next day we experienced another beautiful walk, sometimes resting in the meadows on the side of the path by the shade of old trees. The ground is

1. Rudolf Steiner, *Supersensible Knowledge,* Hudson, NY: Anthroposophic Press, 1987, pp. 156-158.

carpeted with thyme, lavender, and rosemary, so the scent along the path is heavenly. One just wants to sit there and savor the day. The sun shone, but never in our faces as we walked in a southwesterly direction. I always pick up the aromatic plants and put them on my necklace so I can smell the flowers. Lavender is a magic plant, so I put it on my backpack as well. I love the Mediterranean atmosphere, although now we are headed for the Atlantic coast.

> The knowledge we acquire at this sixth stage of [Rosicrucian] initiation is not dry and rational; it forges an intimate connection between ourselves and the greater world. Those who achieve this knowledge are intimately related to everything in the world in a way that modern human beings know only in the mysterious relationship of love between man and woman, which is based on a secret recognition of the being of the other person. Looking at the macrocosm through such a relationship, you not only understand but also feel connected with all beings, just as lovers feel connected. You have an intimate loving relationship to each plant and stone, to all the beings of the world. Our love becomes specialized with regard to each being, which then gives us information it ceased to provide when we descended to modern forms of cognition. Animals eat what is good for them and leave what is harmful; they have a sympathetic relationship to some foods and an antipathetic relationship to others. To develop modern cognition, we humans had to relinquish such

direct relationships, but in future we will regain them on a higher level. How do modern esotericists know that a plant's flower affects human beings differently than its root? How do they know that the effect of an ordinary root is different from that of a carrot? They know because things speak to them just as they also speak to animals. At lower levels, such intimate relationships are incompatible with rational consciousness, but at the highest levels we will enter into such relationships consciously.[1]

🌼

On most walks, one walks to get somewhere, but here it is the land which used to lead to the end of the world or Finistère, or *fini la terre*—end of the earth. In the old days, one walked to the end of the earth as they knew it; after the ocean, the earth ends with abyss. In modern time, the inner abyss must come.

My respect and love of the plants along the way increased with each day. They kept me company and I sang an old song by Simon and Garfunkel that seemed to fit this place. I could have slept on the meadows for the rest of the day, but the gang walked on and so did I. I am reminded of these words from Dante's *Purgitorio*: "The love of god, unutterable and deep flows into a pure soul the way that light rushes into a transparent object. The more love it finds, the more it gives itself, so that,

1. Rudolf Steiner, *The Secret Stream: Christian Rosenkreutz and Rosicrucianism,* Great Barrington, MA: Anthroposophic Press, 2000, p. 77.

A common sight along the way—
note the coquille St. Jacques on the vestments

as we grow clear and open, the more complete the joy of heaven is. And the more souls who resonate together, the greater the intensity of their love, and mirror like, each soul reflects the other."[1]

The next day we decided to have lunch in the larger town of Sahagún and then walk on to Calzadilla de los Hermanillos. The city of Sahagún had a distinct

1. Dante, *Purgitorio* (book xv lines 67–75), in Stephen Mitchell, *The Enlightened Heart: An Anthology of Sacred Poetry,* New York: HarperCollins, 1989.

Arab flavor, with a big market and many Africans sell-
ing their wares. We stopped in the plaza for a meal
and watched people walk around. It was not a very
welcoming atmosphere; I sensed that some of the café
owners were not sympathetic toward the Christian pilgrims. This was the first and only city in which I felt
antagonism toward us as pilgrims. We went on and
found another lovely albergue in a small isolated village, where children were playing in the streets. We
had a great raucous meal at the local bar and laughed
with the few other pilgrims (women from the Midwest,
German men, French couples) who had also taken this
out-of-the-way path.

After a great rest, we got up for the next leg of
the journey to Mansilla de las Mulas. Because I had
walked quite fast and many hours, I probably strained
ligaments in my left knee, which was beginning to ache
and become uncomfortable. I planned to continue anyway, feeling I could not stop. I thought that, after more
than two weeks on the road, my legs had adjusted, but
apparently not. I walked with the gang, and the German
seems to completely lose control when he became cold.
We were having a lunch break and enjoying the sun, but
it was chilly—though us northerners did not mind. We
had sweaters on and were sitting on the cold grass with
the wind blowing on our faces as we ate slowly and
enjoyed our sandwiches. It seemed that the blue-eyed,
cold German blood could not take it. He continued by
himself and doubled his pace, and we just could not follow him; he was merely trying to warm up. As it turned
out, the three of us missed a turn that would have saved
us at least eight kilometers, but we all met again in the

evening. "Blue-eyed" had waited for us and we had not shown up, so he continued to the next town. We all met again for supper in a lovely little city, but now my knee was seriously acting up, so I would have to walk less. I am used to climbing, but the *meseta,* which is quite flat, put more strain on my knee. I had another two to three weeks to go. I no longer felt my backpack, but my knee brought a new level to walking; I could not take a step without feeling some pain, which took some of the joy out of the scenery for me.

We all had an emotional breakfast together for the last time. Smoking Bill had to leave early and rush to Santiago by May 19. It was another 400 kilometers and it was already May 7, which meant walking at least thirty-five to forty kilometers each day. We said good-bye and he continued walking.

We took a bus into León and saw him walking on the path with a beautiful shaman's walking stick from Ecuador and a cigar in his mouth. As I saw him walking alone, I felt guilty for taking the bus, but I do not like to walk in traffic, plus my knee needed a rest.

We arrived in the city of León, and I left the Germans and went on my own. I did not have the patience to wait for them. They had to buy tickets and I was in a hurry to visit the superb Cathedral of León—the Santa María de León Cathedral, also called The House of Light, or *Pulchra Leonina.* I joined them again in the old town and had breakfast. The German girl was going on, so I stayed and walked around with the German man; he would be going to Madrid to catch a plane back to Germany in the morning. We went to the cathedral, and enjoyed the peace and quiet and the magnificent stained glass windows, some of the best I have ever seen. It reminded me of a novel by Bernard Tirtiaux about a master glass painter of the Middle Ages, *Le passeur de lumière*:

> This is the time when the Master Nivard becomes aware of the distance between the vision he had in his mind and how it has been brought to earth, in the material world. It seems to him that he has before him, in this masterpiece, something other than he had envisioned. He feels like a master archer who has missed his target, he would like to find the empty sky again, erase everything, and to start again with an empty window over daylight. His designs which he thought robust and adequate seems to him now without any stability and he finds certain color plays without any grace having lost the magic, fairy effects which he impatiently expected. Besides the enthusiasm which is surrounding him and the fiery compliments of the monks and the passersby, Nivard the Master is worried himself sick. Something has escaped him. Up until now the light has let itself be led by the hand, like an obedient child, but once up there at twenty feet high, far from man's reach, the light is no longer man's friend. Far from up there, the light plays with the master's mind teasingly, the light watches him contemptuously and with insolence. She rejects the Master, and belongs only to herself.
>
> Capricious, cunning, sly, practicing with the illusive fluctuations of time, of transparency and the

seasons to flee endlessly, stained-glass windows is the most savage form of artistic expression, the most unpredictable. The stained-glass window is nothing other than madness, metamorphosis, an illusory blossoming, a play of disheveled wet grass in a river of light.

In the domain of glass and of transparency, the one who thinks himself master is mastered, becomes a slave. During long days, Nivard, the master looks at all the stained-glass windows that he has never made, the colors that he has not chosen, the light which is not what he had intended. He has fits of rage....

Next time, he says to himself with clenched teeth, I will keep you in a tight rein, the bridle will be much tighter. He will keep this unyielding and arrogant beast of the light tight up to the nose. He will leave his iron mark on her forehead. Such is the great challenge of the master painter in glass.[1]

I remained in the cathedral for many hours looking at these exquisite windows, their magic, the play of light. How could anyone have made such magic happen? To me, these stained-glass windows are even better than those in Chartres Cathedral.

The greatest influence on all Christian architecture from the twelfth century on was that of Abbot Suger of Saint Denis (d1151) with his neo-Platonic

1. Bernard Tirtiaux, *Le passeur de lumière,* France: Gallimard, 1995 (translation by Marie Laure Valandro), pp. 334–335.

thought. This abbot, who took as his basis the mysticism of John Scotus Eriugina (d.875) would revolutionize the system of building churches, in which it was necessary to embody the metaphysical theory of light, given its potential for symbolizing. For both of these clergymen, earthly things took part, with logical limitations, in the qualities inherent in the nature of God: goodness, beauty, truth, ranked in a hierarchy in such a way that, starting from the material world, they became a ladder leading up to the immaterial. Visible things are "material lights" which "illuminate" men and allow them to come to the true Light, that is, to God. So, at that very moment, when the glassmaker's art was beginning to be carried out in an industrial way in the area around Paris, the force of symbolism took on an ascensional dimension which was to reach its height in the Gothic cathedrals, especially León. On its doorways, yellowish at dusk, there could have been written, with a fullness of sense, that text immortalized by Suger on the front of the abbey: "What shines out in here is foretold by the golden doorway; through sensual beauty, the soul, still gravid with weight, rises up to true beauty, and from the earth where it lay buried, regains life in Heaven when it beholds the brilliance of these splendours.[1]

I stayed in the little chapel at one side of the cathedral. It is cozier, and the older women usually like to

---

1. Máximo Gómez Rascón, *León Cathedral: The Stained-Glass Windows: Analysis of Subjects,* León, Spain: Edilisa, 2001, p.13.

pray in these little corner chapels. I tried to view the Cathedral at all times of the day to observe how it transforms as the sun moves from east to west and how the different large spaces come to life as the sun shines through them.

> We are not standing before a cold juxtaposition of panes, panels and figures, but before springs of light flowing like blood from a wounded organism. When one looks at the walls, the floor or the vaults of the building, what one sees in each split second is a single dominant hue, always different from the one cast in the previous instant, the fruit of the blending together and mutual symbiosis of coloured volumes in constant movement through the concatenated spaces. In a way we could speak of a capacity for chromatic message, expansive and surprising like the "word of God," which is inexhaustible by its very nature—1000 of individual little pieces of glass, stones, cabochons, precise lines, expressive designs, leaded divisions, hue with their own personalities, individuals with the charm of their own inalienable colour, but which, forgotten each for itself, result in an "almost mystic" communication, of a more fecundating nature.

> This is the root of the cathartic impact produced by the ethereal density of Gothic cathedrals, even on the non-believer, something that is more difficult to achieve if the figurative subjects of the transparent walls are forgone, as is the case with some works of modern art. We stand before

something else, before other contents, before another concept of harmony, of innerness, where all forces are brought into action by the charm of the symbol, until the soul is steeped in the theological copy of the word revealed by the windows themselves, where light and message blend....

Let us not forget that the windows, in the final analysis, are made of powder-dust—just like the most beautiful stones hidden under the ground, also made of worthless matter. These humble components are ennobled by light, which enriches them with the unfathomable gift of their new contents. Without it, things and their hidden messages would doubtless be the slave of darkness, and it is thanks to light that both truth and beauty shine forth, both physically and spiritually.[1]

I was sitting for quite a while deep in admiration of the space and immersed in its magic, having forgotten the German who came into the cathedral with me. I left the little chapel and saw him behind me. He said he was starving and wanted to eat a pizza—a rude awakening to the material world. I meandered through other magic spaces and then waited outside, but somehow he had disappeared. It took about two hours to find each other, by which time I'd had enough of looking and walking around. When I returned to the albergue, I ran into him at the door. I was going to give up looking for him, and he was fuming. Eventually, we headed back into the crowded little center of León and found a lovely

---

1. Ibid., pp. 23–24.

pizzeria, where many other pilgrims were enjoying supper. We enjoyed our evening together, talking about our families and so on. Again, I was becoming a bit sad, as fellow travelers were going their own way; but that is the way of the Camino. Leave the past behind, and move on with thankfulness for what we have been given.

That evening, an old nun of the convent/albergue was leading us in some songs to sing at evening mass. She was like a child in a seventy-five-year-old body (or older). She treated us like children as she gave us direction for the singing. We were all singing the same song but in the different languages. We all enjoyed the singing together and all wished that we could have had some more of this kind of activities. After saying goodbye to the German, I decided to leave. After a full day, we all retired to our crowded dormitories, women on one side and men on the other.

The next morning, when I got up the German was gone. My knee was very sore, even though I had used some of the magic ointment that my friend Marc makes in his small anthroposophical pharmacy in the hills of southern Wisconsin. I had a definite limp now as I put on my backpack and headed for the post office to send a beautiful book on León Cathedral home (the one I just quoted). I took the bus just a few kilometers outside of León and got off. The signs there were very confusing; there were lots of new highways on top of one another, and the Camino signs did not seem to be where they should have been. As a result, I got lost and became upset, because by now I couldn't take a step without pain. Fortunately, a sweet old man on his morning walk showed me the way.

I was once again on track and surrounded by beautiful scenery—not mountains but little hills with the same plants, but becoming dryer with more brush. Cultivation seems to be harder here. I adopted a way of walking that deals with the constant pain. I take each step not anticipating the pain, and I take the pain as it comes because if I anticipate the pain, my whole body tightens up, making the pain far worse. I meet the pain in a relaxed manner; it does not hurt as much, but I'm afraid that I will damage my knee permanently. Perhaps I would not be able to enjoy such extended walks again. So, step-by-step, I walk on.

When I enter Vilar de Mazarife, an inviting albergue stops me. I took off my backpack and sat on the lawn for a deserved rest after all that painful walking. I let the sunshine warm my aching knee and forgot about it all. I took a nap in the sun listening to all the men—Austrians, Germans, Spanish, Dutch and others—talk and sun themselves and heal their bloodied toes, and feet. Later, I went to visit the village and saw the church. Huge stork nests sat on top of the steeples and on anything high. I watched the storks land gently on their nest. During the day I had seen them in the fields and in streams eating frogs. Most of us took a cup of coffee and sat on the stone walls, watching and thoroughly enveloped in the magic of the storks in the orange evening light. Karl König had this to say about these birds:

> The storks are the only birds in this order which at least attempt to draw near to the earth by coming close to man, as the white stork does. They build

their nests on the roofs of houses and stables and return year after year to the old nest. Children love them and expect them to bring them brothers and sisters. And the grown-ups smile at this superstition or condemn this nonsense.

Can we ascribe to this presumption of the intellect the fact that the stork is gradually ceasing to frequent the dwellings of Central and Northern Europe and withdraws ever more from them? We know very well that the stork does not bring our children, but what was it that gave rise to this inner picture for such a long time? Siewert (1955) describes an experience which might perhaps put us on the track of an answer:

In a small Pomeranian town the storks appeared just as school had finished. The children poured out on to the streets, and a little lad who soon spotted the large birds cried out his discovery to the world. All eyes were raised, and all the children laughed at the sight of the long-legged birds in the clear bright sky. But it was not only the children who were glad; many people gazed up from the narrow streets and forgot that only the day before yesterday the last snow had fallen and that the air was still bitterly cold. Even if the people did not sink to their knees at the sight of the storks, as they had done two thousand years ago in honour of the bearers of the spring, at least the joy has remained to this present day, for, just as in ancient times, the wanderers brought the spring to this northerly land, with the sun and warmth of the south, and the long winter with its terror was forgotten.

When Siewert says that the storks were the bearers of spring, he is quite right, but two or three thousands years ago people fell to their knees at the sight of the birds because they knew that with them the souls of unborn children were approaching the earth, and that the time of pairing was beginning. Out of his spiritual insight Rudolf Steiner indicated that, up to the first pre-Christian millennium, births among the Germanic tribes were so arranged that they mostly occurred around the time of Christmas....

The stork's venerable brother, the ibis, was sacred for the ancient Egyptians. They respected it so much that they would embalm the bodies of fallen ibises and flay them in special graves. The death penalty applied to the killing of an ibis, even if this was unintentional. The thrice-great Thoth, whom the Greeks called Hermes Trimegistos, was often represented with the head of an ibis. Even his hieroglyph was a stylized ibis. On his head the Thoth-ibis wore the crescent of the moon, in which the disc of the sun was poised. Thoth was the initiator of Egyptian culture. He was the god of speech and writing and is often represented with a stylus in his hand.

What the ibis was for the Egyptian, the stork became for the peoples of the north. He was wise enough to indicate to them the coming of unborn souls, who were ready to be incarnated on earth. Although, like the swan he wore a white garment, he evoked a quite different image for the soul. His were not powers of the heart but powers of wisdom. To the soul he appeared not perpetually young, like the swan, but old and clever like a midwife.

The swan is connected with that which is gone, the stork with the unborn, with that which has not yet come. Ibis and Thoth were related to the moon....

The stork came every year from the southern-moon-regions of the Lemurian zone up to the North of Europe. Wisdom and humility were balanced in these migrations. The ascending souls of the dead, while on the way to the realm of the sun, were in the regions permeated by the spirit of the swans. The souls returning to earth from the sphere of the moon were related to the storks....

[Storks and swans] are like memory-pictures which have remained alive from a past period of human history. Once they were united with the souls of men. But the earth-substances became hard and impenetrable, and only a few human souls could take up and fill out their bodies. Then came the birds: hard horn grew into their etheric wings, which became earthly organs and made it possible for them to encircle the planet. Nevertheless they remained united with the sun, and thereby with the soul-realm of man.

From then on their destiny took manifold shape and brought them many tasks. Many were lost; others became songsters; many attached themselves to men, as did the chickens, the doves and pigeons. The storks and swans remained connected to the higher part of the human soul. They indicated human destiny: to be born and to die, to be wise but to bear humility in the heart, and one day to become—perhaps—a swan knight. Then the stork will be redeemed.[1]

Watching the storks, which had come from the African continent, was a lovely way to end the evening. I had ordered dinner at the albergue and went back to eat paella, which our host had been preparing all afternoon, sending wonderful aromas throughout the dorm upstairs. The paella was delicious, and the company was equally good. We laughed and joked, even though many of us had one kind of pain or another. Several older Austrian men were in a rare mood of laughter and joking. There were at least seventeen of us from around Europe. Most were men, with just a few women. Later, I found a fat Italian mama's boy in his twenties bathing his soft sore feet in a basin; he had great silk sheets, creams, lotions, and potions, and I wondered how in heaven did he get here.

I will have to walk extremely slowly; I wouldn't be able walk more than fifteen kilometers, twenty at the most. The cook gave me a massage, but the next morning I could barely walk. Nevertheless, I left and after

---

1. Karl König, *Swans and Storks, Sparrows and Doves: Sketches for an Imaginative Zoology,* Edinburgh: Floris Books, 1996, pp. 24-25, 31, 32-33.

two hours of slow walking, my legs warmed up a bit. I walked a while with the Dutch man, with whom I'd had a great conversation at supper. He went on ahead, probably feeling sorry for me. As I approached the village, again I was unable to find the right road and had to go for at least another forty-five minutes on the outskirts of Hospital de Orbigo, trying to find my way and becoming increasingly irate at myself. Being in constant pain, I had a short fuse.

Here I am reminded of the words of José Antonio Garcia Monge:

> El viaje al interior de uno mismo es verdaderamente arriego. No es un viaje facil. Prueba de ello es que muy pocos lo empreden. La mayoria de la humanidad no se atreve a hacer hasta el fondo este viaje al interior de un mismo. Los riegos que bloquean tu decision de caminar hacia ti son, tal vez, encontrarte con alguien que no te gusta, con un desconocido, con zonas oscuras e inexploradas de ti mismo. Este camino no se puede hacer sin atraversar una zona difficil en la que el dolor esta presente como parte de nosotros mismos. No se puede dar a luz una nueva consciencia de uno mismo, un Nuevo autoconcepto, sin dolor. Nos sorprendera tambien el gozo de encontrarnos, de ser unificadamente, pero las crisis de crecimiento que supone este camino interior pasan, frecuentamente, for el dolor de dar a luz.

(The journey within oneself is truly full of perils. It is not an easy journey. The proof of it, is that very few undertake it. Most of us do not venture

Vilar de Mazarife—the chef cooks paella

into this voyage deep within ourselves. The dangers which often block our decision to take this journey are often, something like, being afraid to meet someone we do not care for, the unknown, dark, and unexplored areas deep within ourselves. This walk cannot be undertaken without crossing a difficult zone, one where sufferings and pain are forever present as part of ourselves. One cannot give birth to the light of new consciousness, to new concepts about ourselves without pain. It will surprise us also that we will meet ourselves, and we will be unified, but the crisis of growth which this journey requires is always accompanied by the pain which giving birth to the inner light requires.)[1]

◈

I stopped for lunch in Hospital of Órbigo, which crossed the river; the bridge was magnificent, one of the longest and oldest bridges in Spain, dating from the thirteenth century and built over an earlier Roman bridge, making it one of the great historical landmarks on the Camino.[2] It is ancient, but I did not have the usual interest because of constant pain. I did stop and enjoy the water flowing by and steeped myself in its history, noticing for the first time many tourists and only a few pilgrims.

I continued on and was happy just to be able to walk through the old town. I was thankful that my poor knee, which had clearly been maltreated by not going at my own pace, was still able to take me through these enchanting medieval towns. I bought some food and had lunch on a bench with an older German couple, pilgrims well into their sixties. As I continued along the Camino, the countryside became increasingly hilly— gentle hills with small villages and new home construction here and there. Eventually, I arrived in a kind of abandoned village called Valdeiglesia. The albergue

1. José Antonio Garcia-Monge and Juan A. T. Prieto, *Camino de Santiago: Viaje al Interior de Uno Mismo,* Spain: Editorial Desclee de Brouwer, 1999, p. 21; translation by Marie-Laure Valandro.

2. John Brierley, *A Pilgrim's Guide to the Camino de Santiago,* Forres, Scotland: Findhorn Press, 2006, p. 218.

was in an old stone house not far from the church. It had a lovely, well-tended garden, with yellow-petalled calendula flowers and others that beckoned me to stay. Of course I had little choice, because my knee was too painful. I enjoyed the afternoon in the little garden, sleeping in the grass and chatting with a woman from Southern France and a Dutch woman, who was taking care of the place. It was to be a ladies' afternoon with the obvious female conversations, which I thoroughly enjoyed after being with so many men on the Camino. A rest with women was very welcome. I took a shower outside and enjoyed what remained of the day after massaging my knee with arnica.

An old priest came and checked the place throughout the afternoon, disturbing our friendly chats. He continued to come into the garden with a sour face and bad energy, declining to speak. I had to work hard on myself to avoid returning the same kind of energy, so I ignored him. He is a poor priest, lonely in this little isolated village church, and unable to change with the times. It seemed as though he was looking for bad things in the pilgrims as an excuse to complain about them.

We shared a meal in the evening after a warm, sunny afternoon lazing in the sunshine and chatting, something I had not done until now. It gave me the strength to go on the next day and face the pain.

Next morning, again I could hardly walk, but decided to continue. The scenery was beautiful hills, with farms and tall pine trees and not many people around. I wondered sometimes if I was on the right path. In fact, I did not get lost, but just walked slowly and enjoyed the panorama. I went past old farms and farmers getting on their tractors to work the fields. It always reminds me of fields seen from an airplane; they look marvelous from 20,000 or 30,000 feet up, and we can truly see the work of the farmers—their well-tended fields show up neat and well cared for and in various colors, depending on what is growing. We see the amount of work needed to tend and cultivate the land, but we often forget about it even though our lives depend on farmers. I am always thankful when I see them ready for the day's work. Farmers always have the look of the land on their body and features. They seem to grows with the land; hands become sinuous, the body strong and tanned, and the face, hardened by the elements but softened by the love of the earth. Farmers are a vanishing breed, but here in these remote villages, they continue to work their fields. Farther up the path, an old man was taking his morning stroll through his land, checking the plants, the trees, loving his land with his faithful dog following him. We chatted and then parted. This part of the path is very isolated, and sometimes I wondered if this was the right place. Eventually, I encountered a kind of shrine with funny sculptures and saw that this was indeed the path. I walked through a beautiful forest and then descended toward the town of Astorga. I am reminded of these words from Georg Kühlewind:

One element is hidden within all spontaneous uncognitive emotions, through which they are "feelable," and through which they make themselves known as specific emotions, a manisfesting force which is, however, enchanted in muteness:

it does not say anything, announces itself only as a perceptible call for understanding. Emotions are surging against the one who feels them, like a pressure, or blow, not like a word. If the one who is feeling the emotions would meet them with receptive thinking attention, he could supplement them with what they are lacking, they became uncommunicating and certain feelings which pull, push and press instead of speaking to man. Within this mute urging one can discover the living light, denying itself within this urge. Participation in this light is the original pure joy. Therefore one can say that in every emotion, pure joy is waiting to be released by man out of its enchantment.

The "warm" power, which lives in genuine thinking, allowing it to "penetrate" the phenomena of the world, is the objective receptive feeling. It can also be called "pure" feeling. In its denial—the metamorphosis into mute emotions—this feeling is fixed. Therefore, every emotion that overwhelms us, is a question, a possibility, a gate which can open and lead us to joy, to seeking, to questioning, receptive pure feeling.

This is the meaning of pain: it signalizes the call for change; when pain is not present in the course of an illness, the illness is not noticed, or only late. This means for the domain of the soul that painless sinning, which accepts what is not good, has been accepted as part of the Ego.[1]

---

1. Georg Kühlewind, *Thinking with the Heart,* Fair Oaks, CA: Rudolf Steiner College Press, pp. 54–55.

⚜

My legs had warmed up, and I could put up with the pain. Again I was trying to walk without apprehension of the pain, but trusting each step, trying not to anticipate the pain and wince before each step. Just walk, dissipate the pain with trust. It worked quite well, while I walked, and after two hours it was fine. Stopping, however, was a problem. I am nevertheless very glad that I can keep walking, even in this way.

I arrived in Astorga after a bit of confusion. I saw my favorite companions, whom I had lost—the Italian artist and the Austrian teenager. It was good to say hello to them, and they enjoyed seeing me. I had come to think that everyone had disappeared. I was kind of like their mother.

I found a hostel with lots of atmosphere and great music, and I stayed there. It is close to the closed cathedral and its gardens and stone benches. I enjoyed looking at the old stone-relief work and simply enjoyed sitting, since I could not run all over town as I usually do, which was unfortunate, since this town is very rich in history and beautiful buildings. However, I had to rest my knee if I wanted to go on. I still had 230 kilometers or more to go. This second part of my Camino includes the pain element, and it changed the way that I perceived the path. I am just thankful to be on my legs and no longer run around to see what else I can cram into this trip. I am forced to slow down and refrain from running enthusiastically from church to church. I have to slow down, and rest, which is difficult for me. I realize, too, that I am the last one and perhaps will not finish the walk. I had not considered the possibility of getting hurt at all. So here I am, pushing the limits of my body, because I did not listen to it when it said, slow down now. Let the others run in front. I ran with them and now I pay the price. When walking this Camino, I read of course, you must keep at your own pace.. but that is quite difficult when everyone is excited, walking fast, talking, laughing, enjoying. I just kept going, knowing that the inner voice was right in telling me to slow down. It is sometimes difficult to pace oneself, when one meets others who have been walking for only one or two weeks. Most of us take six or seven weeks or even three months of intense walking everyday, and we must walk differently than someone who is just here for a few days. They may walk faster, because they will be home soon; for those of us on the long run, however, we must rest and measure our efforts, which I did not do.

I sat in the lovely hostel since I could not run around and read comments by some of the pilgrims. I heard Pierre say, "Merci pour l'accent, tu as fait de cette maison une belle acceuillante qui sourit a tous les caminos, a l'image de la lumière de Saint-Jacques. Que la force soit avec vous." (Thanks for atmosphere that you created in this old home. It is welcoming and smiles to all the Camino, in the image of the light of St. Jacques… may the power be with you.) Peter (from Scotland): "May all people, all religions walk the earth together as one loving energy! Om mani padme hum!" There were many others.

Now as I sit in this lovely place, it was a kind of magic to be walking with all these people whom I hardly knew, but they fitted so well with the scenery. Everyone walks the same road, sometimes together, and sometimes we lose sight of some and we meet them again. We meet one another on the path with a great warm camaraderie. Women and men—we meet one another with the same enthusiasm. I had many laughs during those last few days. Sometimes I said nothing for hours and just walked. I was just content to be and see what was around with no need to say anything. I had great times, walking with others or alone and truly tasting what the path had to bring, whether adorable or poor, dilapidated villages, old chapels with big closed wooden doors, blue skies, fields of lavender, grapevines, sage, rosemary, red dirt paths undulating in the distances, steeples showing up in the distant horizon, daisies, and lots of poppies who seem to send kisses from heaven ("Las flores nos dan un beso," as the Mexican doctor pilgrim said), relaxing coffee breaks in the middle of the day, lunch stop in the flowered fields, evening dinner, and rowdy sleepless nights in crowded sonorous snoring quarters.

I laughed about nothing and just enjoyed the hours as they came. I wanted this to last forever—who would not? However, practical life returns, and so it was the end of this part of the Camino. What is the lesson? We cannot have some happiness without paying for it somehow. I had pain in the knee, and the woman who gave me a massage at the albergue said to me, "The left knee indicates lack of humility." I pondered on that. Where was my lack of humility? I am definitely learning now, being very humble about my walking capabilities. I do not know if I will even finish this walk.

Now I am walking alone. The companions on the first half of the trip have disappeared, gone home or just ahead, but I will surely meet another bunch around the corner. Now it is time out for reconsidering things—thanks to the knee!

This Camino reminds me of the road to the East, from Europe, via Greece, Turkey, Iran, Afghanistan, Pakistan, India and that young people traveled in the 1960s and 1970s. The road was opened, then and hippies and backpackers going around the world crisscrossed those countries. The Camino, however, is truly superb. It seems we are all on the same wavelength. The Dutch woman back at the albergue talked about higher energies, living with higher beings and so on. I felt this way when I was meditating during ten-day retreats in the Burmese Vipassana Buddhist tradition. It was the same place that we all reached but by sitting down. Sitting silently all day from 6:00 am to 10:00 pm, not talking, not looking anyone in the eyes; total silence for ten days, listening to discourses and practicing spiritual exercises to control and silence the overactive mind. After such a retreat, we would be in another space by having closed our senses to the outside world and trying to control our dissipated thinking and attain one-pointed mind.

Here, it is the opposite, but we live in that same space I had acquired in the Buddhist retreats. Here the senses are all open, all day. Instead of closing the senses, we open them fully to the world outside—the sky, the trees, clouds, flowers, mountains, churches, people, trees, old paths, and old roads. Our senses get their fill by the end of the day, and then we go on, filled to the brim with new experiences, new friends, new relationships, new scents, new vistas, new valleys, and new plateaus. Women and men are not separated, but live and sleep side-by-side, eat together, and walk together.

It seems that now I have traveled both paths, the Eastern and the Western. I have tasted both and see what each has to offer. However, I find we all enter the same land. Where is that land?

I was just hoping that my knee would heal a bit and allow me to continue walking. I give thanks everyday to my legs for carrying me in these beautiful places. I took that for granted when I started, but no longer. I truly appreciate where my legs are bringing me and that I am just happy to be on this path. Tonight I will cook a meal with Elisa, a good Italian meal. She went shopping and returned with enough for a feast, so we stuffed ourselves with salads, olives, spaghetti, red wine, bread, and dessert.

The music played, and I was reminded of my twenty-four-year-old son and nineteen-year-old daughter and their dad. I would love to do this walk with them, but they would leave me in the dust; they are more fit than I am. It would be a nice family journey for the future.

One question that comes to mind is this: How can we maintain a state of being permanently in love with everything and everyone without appearing to be mad? There is a certain magic on the Camino; everyone we meet, regardless of age, or sex, race or anything, brings an instant warmth. One gains a fresh outlook and love of the moment, love of the day not yet born, love of the day that just ended and leaving its tales to share. How do we take that home?

These words from the Psalms seem related to the situation:

> Blessed are the man and the woman
> Who have grown beyond their greed
> And have put an end to their hatred
> And no longer nourish illusion.
> But they delight in the way things are
> And keep their hearts open, day and night.
> They are like trees planted near flowing rivers,
> Which bear fruits when they are ready.
> Their leaves will not fall or wither
> Everything they do will succeed.[1]

I decided to have a massage to try to improve my injured knee. After a Reikei massage, the woman tried to help me by saying, "You love details; you look at people, the details, and of course you do not like what you see. You miss the whole point." I realize that am not generous and not soft enough. I must become softer. I am too hardened. The left knee relates to humility, love of self, devotion to the self. That is what she said. This is what I have to work on for the rest of this Camino. As I step painfully, I am forced to look at something else. What?

I started again the next day, heading again for the mountains to Rabanal, a lovely hill village situated at 3500 feet and having the twelfth-century Romantic Chapel of Santa Maria, with monks in the adjacent monastery where pilgrims can stay. However, I stayed

---

1. The Book of Psalms, from Stephen Mitchel, *The Enlightened Heart: An Anthology of Sacred Poetry,* New York: HarperCollins, 1989.

in another albergue. I walked with more difficulty today, even with my pep talk about melting the pain. Finally, I hitched a ride with a lonely passing salesman, who took me to the next town. In the car, I passed all of my friends, and my heart was aching. The Mexican doctor, the Italian girl, and others were climbing through an oak and pine forest; Smoking Bill and the German girl are three days ahead. It was tough to swallow—defeat or whatever—seeing my friends walk. I did walk twelve kilometers with the old German couple, but I do not know how. Now the pain is too much and I can't walk. I feel guilty for not having listen to my body.

I love the monastery, and at eight o'clock many of us are going to the church service. It is a nice service with a handful of monks from a Benedictine monastery in Germany trying to live in this little town to reawaken the meditative life. They also offer rooms to pilgrims who want to join them in their monastic life for a few days, both men and women. I think that is a big step toward living in the twenty-first century. The little village had lovely atmosphere, and a beautiful big old flowering chestnut tree by the chapel was giving us some well-deserved shade. The cool chapel was home to a great silence between its thick walls. One could feel the smell of intense meditative life.

> In earlier ages communicating with the divine spiritual worlds could only be brought about through the use of mantras and sound. Today, through words filled with meaning and content, man can prepare the way in his inner being with the union with the Christ force. When the pupil succeeds

in entirely shutting himself off in his meditation from external infuences and noise, when he is able to eliminate the physical body, he is then living only in the etheric body, astral body and ego. Something like a magnet fluid must draw us across into the spiritual worlds in our meditation; then we are on the right path. It is not the words themselves that matter, but that the right meaning and content should stream into us as a life-awakening force from the spiritual worlds, that they should be filled with meaning through the Christ force. The words of the meditation formulae are chosen in such a way that they work quite impersonally; they are garment in which the Logos streaming through the world can clothe itself.

Something of the utmost importance takes place in selfless meditation; through this intimate process of meditation, a fine consumption of warmth is produced. Every meditation is linked with a delicate warmth and light process. Warmth and light are used up by us when we meditate and this gives rise to a life-process. In our ordinary thinking a warmth process also takes place in our organism and this brings about memory. It must not come to this, however during meditation. If we live in pure thought-content, then what we consume inwardly of warmth and light is not impressed into our body but into the general cosmic ether. And this causes an external process in our surroundings. During a genuine meditation we impress the form of our thought upon the universal ether: and if in our retrospection we observe a meditation process, we are not confronted with a memory but with an objective perception of the imprints in the cosmic ether.

One who engages in true meditation is living in a process which is at the same time a world process: What takes place is the following. In meditating, warmth is consumed and therefore cold ensues; the universal ether is cooled down. And since light, too, is consumed, it is dimmed down, darkness ensues. It is always possible to a clairvoyant to tell if a person has meditated somewhere; a shadow-image of him remains behind which is actually cooler than the surroundings. Something has been effected which one can compare with the print on a photographic plate.

If we reflect upon this we shall be able to understand how someone returning to earth in his following earthly life still finds traces of his meditation thoughts in the cosmic ether. Here we have a concrete example of the working of karma. The meditator comes more and more to the feeling: it is not merely you, with your thoughts; something transpires into which no doubt you are placed, but it goes on outside you as something that remains. This "feeling of oneself as in the atmosphere of the weaving and being of one's thoughts," as if thoughts move through us like waves, gives us a definite feeling. It is the assured feeling that one stands in a spiritual world and is oneself but a weaving member in the general weaving of the divine world. And it is a remarkable feeling that then comes over us in the stillness of the soul: it is not you alone that creates that—it is created! You have begun to stir these waves but they spread themselves out around you. They have a life of their own of which you are but the center.

The most important, significant moments for our development in our esoteric life are those *after* the meditation, when we let absolute calm enter our soul in order to allow the content of the meditation to work upon it. We must strive to extend these moments more and more, for through this "lifting ourselves" out of the circle of our everyday thoughts and feelings, through the "emptying itself" of our soul, we unite with a world from which pictures come toward us, pictures that we can compare with nothing out of our usual life.

If after every meditation we awaken in ourselves a feeling of gratitude and awe—a feeling that we can call a mood of prayer—and are conscious at the same time of the grace in which we have participated, we shall realize that we are on the right path and that the spiritual worlds come toward us.[1]

🌰

I went to eat in the local restaurant and met up again with the Brazilians, Italians, and Mexicans. One of the

1. Rudolf Steiner, *Guidance in Esoteric Training: From the Esoteric School,* London: Rudolf Steiner Press, 2001, pp. 166, 168.

Brazilians is a huge man; one of his hands is as big as my face. I give him a lot of credit, because being so big and overweight must make it painful to walk. He never complains, though; he is always jovial and kind, never saying why he is walking the Camino. He comes from Brazil, where he worked as an engineer in the oil industry.

I did not walk alone for long. We were all a rowdy bunch with the local Spaniards who were looking at the soccer game on television. The evening was one of laughter and shared stories from home and the Camino, and a few pilgrims got a bit drunk. Returning to the hostel, I noticed a priest chatting with the pilgrims. He was young and Nordic in appearance—one of us, but with the traditional black robe that always places a barrier between him and others. Pilgrims are trying to reconnect their spiritual life with daily life. The priest has a spiritual life and then a daily life, with moments for prayer and services and time for other daily activities such as eating, washing, and the like. We pilgrims, on the other hand, tried to make every moment sacred; not just one or two hours a day, but the whole day. Walking the path helped us do that. All the minutes became special and sacred. That seemed to be the difference between the black-robed monk and us.

The next part of the trip was the famous Cruz de Fero and Mount Irago, at 5000 feet. Every one was preparing for the long ascent.

Rabanal del Camino continues a centuries-old tradition of caring for the pilgrims before they take the steep path up and over Monte Irago (Mount

*In Manjarín, a well-known town with lots of character,
between Rabanal del Camino and Molinaseca*

Rabanal). This was the ninth stage of Aymeric Picaud's classic itinerary, and the Knights Templar are thought to have had a presence here as early as the twelfth century, ensuring the safe passage of pilgrims over this remote terrain—the Church of Santa Maria was possibly built by them.[1]

The next day, I got up again and was going to take a cab, but it was too expensive, so I waited for a ride. None came, so I walked again—very painful, but after the usual two hours, the muscles or ligaments or tendons warmed up. I am going into the mountains again, so it is easier; I'm using knee ligaments different from

---

1. John Brierley, *A Pilgrim's Guide to the Camino de Santiago*, Forres, Scotland: Findhorn Press, 2006, p. 234.

those used on flat terrain. I arrived in Molinaseca after walking about fifteen kilometers. I was grateful for the climbing, which saved me. The view goes on forever, waves of mountains after mountains appear in the distance. It seems a truly wild territory, with a wonderful wind on my face and a nice warm sun. Everyone walks slowly with frequent stops. It is a long climb requiring attention and endurance. I am walking better now, even passing others. I found that I could climb, but couldn't walk well on flat terrain.

> Climb the mountains and get their good tidings, Nature's peace will flow into you as sunshine flows into trees. The winds will blow their own freshness into you, and the storms their energy, while cares will drop off like autumn leaves.[1]

I stopped in Foncebadon, a tiny semi-abandoned hamlet and a well-known hippy enclave. I had a coffee there and chatted with other pilgrims while looking at the lovely mountains stretching into the far distance. It looks as though it would be harsh terrain in the winter. The hippies here seemed to be living in the previous century, but I enjoyed their down-to-earth hardiness and strength in turning their backs on the materialistic world in this tough, lonely, magnificent setting. These mountains are remote, but the people are hardy and warm.

Again I had to cope with major pain. I taught myself how to walk with the pain, placing my feet as lightly

---

1. John Muir, from Jim Dale Vickery, *Wilderness Visionaries: Leopold, Thoreau, Muir, Olson, Murie, Service, Marshall, Rutstrum,* Minocqua, WI: NorthWord Press, 1994.

In Molinaseca—nursing a painful knee

as possible on the ground to limit impact on the knee and ligaments, walking with love. If I stomped my feet down, the way I did for the first four weeks, the shock would go from the ground into the knee, even though I had two walking sticks and bandages on each knee. I realized that I had walked without much love for my legs. I was forced to honor my legs; the secret is to walk softly and with love with every step, almost not touching the ground.

What did this teach me for life in general? I am not gentle enough. These verses express something of this:

> Ten thousand flowers in spring, in autumn the moon, a cool breeze in summer, snow in winter. If your mind is not clouded by unnecessary things, this is the best season of your life. (WU-MU)

The birds have vanished from the sky
And now the last clouds drain away
We sit together, the mountains and me
Until only the mountains remain. (LI-PO)

God is a pure no-thing
Concealed in now and here;
The less you reach for him,
The more he will appear. (SILESIUS)

He who binds to himself a joy
Does the winged life destroy.
But he who kisses the joy as it flies
Lives in eternity's sunrise. (WILLIAM BLAKE)[1]

I walked up and down the mountains in very unforgiving terrain, and going downhill had become too much. After a few kilometers I looked for a ride, and a man with his son picked me up and took me to Molinaseca. It was a long, winding road to the next city, and we passed many little villages that I would like to have visited and explored. I must return one day and do this place justice.

I was unable to visit the sights in the town, and I had to stay in the albergue and eat unappetizing food. However, it was a nice evening with many people coming in, including a number of Italian women cycling the Camino and looking very fit, and a retired dentist from Finland, with whom I had occasionally walked. She

---

1. In Stephen Mitchell, *The Enlightened Heart: An Anthology of Sacred Poetry*, New York: HarperCollins, 1989.

was a strong-looking woman with the aura of a warm, Nordic mother in her sixties. She was a great walker enjoying her retirement. The Dutch man also arrived and observed the evening spectacle from his top bunk bed. I chatted with many French pilgrims. One couple, with whom I'd walked occasionally, was having a hard time; the man had heart problems and insisted on walking on this difficult part of the Camino. He arrived late and went straight to bed. An affectionate and friendly couple, they are retired and living in southern France.

The next day I rose early and, after walking a couple of kilometers, realized I would need to hitch another ride to the bus station to get me through the next stage. I could no longer walk. This time my ride took me to the bus station for my next leg of the journey, giving me a rather quick view along the route to Ponferrada, which included the famous twelfth-century Castillo de los Templarios (Castle of the Knights Templar), with its towers and the famous church of the Oak tree (la encina). There are many things to see, so I will return one day.

I waited at the bus station with other pilgrims who appeared to have the problems like my own, many of them limping or suffering bad toes, like the woman from Quebec, who was waiting for her husband. We had a nice chat about Chicoutimi, Quebec, so far away. At this point, we have all walked at least 400 kilometers, and things happen. The bus station is where you meet casualties of the Camino.

It is not so bad, though, because it will make me return to see what I have missed in this part of Galicia. The bus took me into the old town of Villafranca del

Looking ahead to the state of Galicia

Bierzo, passing a beautiful countryside of hills, farms, oak trees, meadows, and fertile land. As I sat on the bus, I could see pilgrims in the distance walking with their backpacks and sticks, and I felt a knot in my throat. I would not be able to finish the Camino the regular way, being unable to walk the required twenty-five kilometers each day to reach Santiago on time. I will walk wherever the path climbs, and when it descends, I will hitch a ride.

I got off the bus and found the albergue someone had mentioned as a funky place to stay, and, thank goodness, the way went uphill. It was a Sunday morning, so I put everything on my bed in the dorm and went walking—no, hobbling—around. I bought lots of food—salami, bread, cheese, pastries, cream of chestnut, and juice. I met up with friends who had kept going, including the older French men I had met a week earlier. I had a lively discussion for a couple of hours with Paul, and we shared a meal together. Paul is a French man who was cycling from Bretagne and on his way to Portugal and the sacred site of Fatima. He had been a maraîcher (a truck farmer) who had become bitter and disillusioned about his wife but loved his grandson. We had supper together and enjoyed each other's company for the evening. A charming man, he was a poet, writer, and lover of good music.

We went to bed quite early and in the morning said goodbye. He said that he would send me the video of his travels when it was finished. He was making it for the people of his town, both young and old.

After a light breakfast, I arranged for a ride up the valley to the place where I would start hiking. I would go without my backpack, and someone would take it to the top of the mountain, the famous O Cebreiro. The first few kilometers were arduous, but then it started to climb and I could manage. The forest was very old, and one could feel the history and that it was an important place. It was peaceful and the mountain steep. It was hot and we went slowly, with everyone perspiring. After climbing a while, and, after crossing a beautiful old bridge, I stopped at the quiet village of Herrerías. I had a breakfast of omelet and fresh bread that the baker had just delivered to a restaurant in a renovated stone house along the path. The village is tucked away in little valleys between the mountains, with a lovely stream flowing through it.

I started climbing again and reached another village on top of a ridge. I stopped there along with several other pilgrims. Surrounded by fabulous scenery, in the

*Villafranca del Bierzo—French man from Bretagne
biking on a round trip to Fatima*

far distance we could see the mountains of Galicia. We
were now leaving the province of Castile y León. The
mountains here seemed very old and had been mined
long ago for silver. Among the huge walnut trees, old
stone farmhouses were being renovated, no doubt by
foreigners. A local farmer and gardener gave me a
handful of walnuts. I sat and enjoyed the scenery and
watched a couple of farmers work the side of the mountain, plowing their fields with horses the way it has been
done for hundreds of years. It is very difficult to get
to these places; there's hardly any road, and we saw

Looking back at Castile y León

villages even farther up in the mountains, in more isolated places where the pilgrims do not go. Many cows were grazing in the fields, and we could hear their bells sounding in the distant valleys.

After a great rest, I climbed again toward the top of this beautiful path. Many people dread walking up this steep mountain, but it made walking possible for me. I felt fortunate that I could even see this, so I thanked my luck.

I stopped again, because now I could see the village where I would spend the night. It was still early, so I had another snack—this time in a meadow overlooking the mountains and in the company of a Spanish man who was bicycling and obviously quite taken by the scenery. We had a chat, and he shared the fact that he and his wife could not have children. Cycling here is an arduous task and probably more difficult than walking.

On the climb to O Cebreiro,
entering Galicia—what a relief!

Eventually, I arrived on top of the famous Cebreiro. The hill has a certain Celtic atmosphere, and in these far-off mountains of Galicia, we enter another kind of atmosphere. Apparently, this place was too remote to be influenced by the Romans, and the invading Saracens were unable to make it up into these complicated waves of mountains. The people of the northern countries must have arrived here and populated it in the distant past. They left their deep spiritual influences, which have survived until today.

> Celtic Christianity is a wonder; among all the attempts to embody the Christian message it is unique; and yet it arises so naturally, so spontane-ously, out of what came before that one cannot tell where it begins and where what came before, which was presumably pagan, ends....

Legends speak to the history of this understanding. There is the story for instance, that Ireland existed before the Fall, as the image of Paradise on Earth, so that when the rest of the earth fell with humanity and received fallen humanity as its partner and fellow pilgrims, Ireland remained as it were unfallen, a place apart, still an image of Paradise on Earth. Here we have an explanation, in picture form, of how and why such high wisdom concerning humanity, the cosmos, and the divine—reaching back to Paradise and forward to the future evolution of the earth—was able to be preserved and transmitted to Ireland. No wonder, too, that Paradise or original nature is more clearly discernible in Ireland....

No wonder therefore that we can find no beginning for Christianity in Ireland. It was always here. From the moment of Golgotha, the new dispensation was growing and the sacrificial task of the Celtic Church was laid down: to develop a true, whole Christianity and carry it eastward into Europe to seed the spiritual culture of the future. And so, as we follow the stream of Celtic Christianity from the Hibernian Mysteries, through the historical saints of Ireland—Brigid, Patrick, Columba, Columbanus, Scotus Eriugena and countless others—we see this Celtic spirit metamorphosing, inspiring, and infusing all that is valuable in our spiritual history.

Out of this church, deeply involved in transmuting the ancient Mysteries out of the wisdom of the vast sweep of evolution and history, arose a veritable army of saints, holy men and women, mystics and magicians, scholars and true philosophers. These were at first only in Ireland, but then as the sense of mission ripened, they began to go *peregrinatio pro Christi*—"wandering for Christ," seeking "white martyrdom"—across the waters of Europe, where they laid down the material, and spiritual conditions for the metamorphoses of the human soul.[1]

⬡

I was deeply thankful to these wondering pilgrims from more than a thousand years ago who brought their great heritage from so far away. I had the feeling that I was in Ireland; Celtic music played in the tourist stores and Celtic art was everywhere in the beautifully maintained village. Of course this place had many tourists; they arrived from the northern side in buses that climbed slowly up the mountain. I enjoyed hobbling about in the hill town with its cobblestone paths and restored stone houses. The old chapel was small and quiet, a great place to sit and enjoy the mood. I had not been a tourist on the Camino thus far, so today I played the tourist that day and bought a local music CD.

Cebreiro had numerous terraces on which to sit and fill our senses with the magical scenery. As my friends arrived one by one, we all sat down to drinks, and the Italians who were cycling began to get quite drunk. As

1. Christopher Bamford, *The Voice of the Eagle: The Heart of Celtic Christianity,* Great Barrington, MA: Lindisfarne Books, 2000, pp. 23–24, 30–31.

the sun was setting, we gazed into the distant hills we would have to cross on the way to Santiago, 160 kilometers ahead.

The following offers more insights into this area of Spain, which feels very different from where I just came from. The difference in atmosphere is palpable, even in the mountains themselves.

> The *Celtic* tribes very early had closer relations with the *Iberians,* the ancestors of the *Basque* people, the oldest inhabitants of the Iberian Peninsula. These Iberians were so closely allied with the Celtic people that the historians of classical antiquity spoke of so-called Celt-Iberians as a mixture of Celtic and Hiberian tribes. Celtic people must have lived in Western Europe long before the sixth century B.C....

> Again let us draw attention to those ancestors of the Basques, the Hiberians. Some old form of that most ancient European vernacular may have been the idiom first spoken in Britain and Ireland.

> Are any Basque words to be found in English? There are more than we imagine. There are English words which hardly can be connected with any European linguistic group except with Basque, such as the common word *key.*

The word-stem key *in English and in Basque*

English	Anglo-Saxon	Old Frisian	Basque
Key	Caeg, Caeg-e	Kai, Kei (key)	Gak-o (key)

With only the exception of Old Frisian the word *key* is not encountered in any other of the Germanic or Indo-European vernaculars except in English and in Basque.

The word for key *in other Indo-European tongues.*

German	Latin	French	Old Greek	Russian
Schlüssel	Clav-is	Clef	Kleis	Klyuch

Through Basque, as often happens in ancient idioms, we are able to discover the original meaning of *KEY*, Anglo-Saxon *CAEG-e*. Basque, *KHAK-o* means hook, and a key was originally a sort of hook.

There are words such as *LAND* common to the whole Teutonic circle and to some Celtic vernaculars, lacking in all the other Indo-European tongues, but found in Basque. *land* is a very old word found in country names such as Eng*land*, Scot-*land*,Ire-*land*, Ice-*land*, Hol*land*, Fin*land*, Switzer*land*, most of them countries located in the vicinity of the Hibernian or Hiberian region

The word-stem LAND in the Germanic group.

Anglo-Saxon	English, Dutch, German	Old Norse, Gothic	Swedish
Land, Lond	Land	Land	Land

of the European west-coast. The word however is lacking in Latin, Greek, and Slavic, in India, Persia, and

Armenia as well as in other parts of the Old world. Only in French do we find LAND-e (heath, moor) presumably borrowed from some Celtic dialect or Germanic dialect. Finally, we meet the word in Celtic vernaculars and in Basque.

The word-stem LAND in Celtic dialects and in Basque.

Basque	Irish	Welsh	Breton	French
Lann (land)	Lann (land, church)	Llann (open place)	Lann, Lan (land)	Land-e (heath)

.... Words are keys to the mysteries of the past. The word *land* can open still other doors. English students both of anthropology and linguistics, expressed the opinion that the first invaders may have landed in the British Islands as early as about 7000 B.C. Who were the invaders who penetrated France and Spain in so remote epochs? Were they perhaps the same people who left us masterworks such as the ceiling-paintings of the Franco-Cantabrian caves, those of Altamira in Spain and Trois Freres in Southern France? Whence did they come, from the West, East, or North? Let us take the word *LAND* and see where there may be further links. In Gaulish we discover *land-a* (land) just as in Basque the form *land-a* (land). The shorter form, *LAN* can be found across the Atlantic, in Mexico: *LAN* (land, country, place) preserved in country names such as Tu-*lan,* Azt-*lan,* Tlapal-*lan.*

The word-stem LAND, LAN
in Indo-European, Basque, American.

Mexican	Basque	Breton	English	Gaulish	Welsh
Lan	Land-a	Lan(n)	Land,	Land-a	Llann
(land)	(land)	(territory)	Lane	(land)	(yard)

.... Some light has been shed on (the beginning of English) by taking into consideration the Basque tongue as representing an early language possibly spoken in the British Isles.[1]   •

❧

The albergue was not so great, but at least I had a bed. I met up with the Italian girl and her boyfriend and their new companions who had come from Madrid to meet her, and the Brazilians and the Dutch man and another tall German and a young American kid from Michigan, who was on his way to South Africa to do humanitarian work. We all had a raucous evening dinner at one of the local restaurants. The Brazilians and Italians had many bottles of red wine on their tables. I sat at the northern blood table, which was filled with glasses of beer. We watched the evening die into sunset colors from the top of the O Cebreiro, the second highest point on this journey, at 4300 feet. After much laughter, we all went to our bunk beds.

Here I am reminded of the words by Mechtild of Megburg:

---

1. Arnold D. Wadler, *One Language: Source of All Tongues*, Great Barrington, MA: Lindisfarne Books, 2006, pp. 33–37.

Effortlessly
Love flows from God to Man
Like a bird who rivers the air
Without moving her wings.
Thus we move in his world
One in body and soul,
Though outwardly separate in form.
As the source strikes the notes
Humanity sings.
The holy spirit is our harpist
And all strings
Which are touched by love
Must sound.[1]

In the morning I got up at seven o'clock and started to walk slowly through meadows and trees, gradually descending. After about seven kilometers, I stopped on the main road and waited for a shop to open so I could get breakfast, since I had had nothing to eat. Nothing was opening, however, and there were no cars on the road, so hitchhiking was out of the question. I continued to walk along the road, going back up through beautiful Galician hills. Tiny farms could be seen in the distance, and there were livestock here. I finally stopped for lunch in the town of Hospital de la Condesa. By now, I was seriously hungry. It was a lonely spot, and the dark-haired waitress was pleasant. I was surprised to see the Brazilians having lunch there.

Since I had no choice I had to continue the best I could. This time the road went up and the pain was

1. Stephen Mitchell, *The Enlightened Heart: An Anthology of Sacred Poetry,* New York: HarperCollins, 1989.

less. Nevertheless, it was a hot and sweaty climb up to the Alto de Poio pass at 1330 meters (4400 feet), higher than the O Cebreiro. From the top, sitting outside and sipping coffee, I was able to rest my knee and look out at both sides of the pass and the fantastic views of Galicia on one side, which was where I was headed, and on the other, where I had come from: the distant mountains of Castile and León and the faraway *meseta*.

The restaurant was bustling with activity and cars were passing on the road. Quite a few pilgrims were resting after the climb and preparing for the ten-kilometer descent into the town of Triacastela (three castles). I decided again to go slowly to the next town. The scenery was so enchanting that I could not bring myself to hitch a ride, plus the expansive scenery helped take away the pain. I walked and walked, looking at the beautiful panorama unfolding below, arriving in Fonfría after 3.3 kilometers. There I determined that it would not be too expensive to get a taxi to take me the rest of the way to Triacastela. I took off my shoes and sat outside on a wall while waiting for my ride. At least I had seen some striking scenery—one step at a time.

An old man drove the taxi over a beautiful winding road and into Triacastela. This town is a little larger and in a valley with a river flowing through it. The guidebook tells me that the stones used to build the Cathedral de Santiago—now only eighty-eight miles away—were quarried here.

It was a warm day, so I did my wash and spent the rest of the day lounging lazily with other pilgrims. I met up again with the Québecquois couple, the Italian artist, and various new faces. The mountains are beautiful here and the people poorer, but the valley is quiet and restful. The river flows past the albergue, and the town has some lovely churches. However, I stayed close to the albergue to rest my knee and prepare for the next day. Nearby was a place where I could get a massage. I went for it, hoping it would help my knee, which it did.

I found a lovely talk published by Parroco Augusto Losada Lopez, the local priest of the church, entitled "Camino de Santiago—the human spiritual dimension; spirituality, culture Trekking or tourism or holiday?"

> The "Camino" was born from the faith of our ancestors who were seeking something; the clear aim of faith is to express our inner selves, the life within us, culture! Logically, the Camino expresses the faith within us. They complement each other in the Camino. We are speaking about the culture of the Camino de Santiago, which is an expression of the faith. Trekking, tourism, I do not deny that a pilgrim begins the Camino without knowing what they are doing, and then also to know themselves. They can get to know Jesus Christ. The Camino is not a holiday or trekking or tourism, even though the pilgrim begins the Camino in this way.
>
> Holidays! They can be enjoyed, but the Camino is not designed as a vacation, although the human being can learn things on vacation. It has or we have to be always in the attitude of searching. The Camino is *universality;* the Camino is universal without exclusive identities. We all feel as one, and each traveler experiences a small universal

*Ermita-refugio de San Nicolás—
statue of St. Thomas*

fraternity. You can find fellowship; through shared vision, projects, plans, you can live among equal others.

It is an interior way of knowing oneself, being capable of discovering the capacity that we have through sharing ourselves with others. It is about searching and meeting. Searching oneself, because sometimes we are strangers and we can find Jesus Christ. It is also a time to consider our values,

*Ermita-refugio de San Nicolás—the priest
who looks after the pilgrims (with French woman)*

which can get lost in the train and travail of life.
It means doing realistic and feasible tasks and not
feeling overwhelmed by life. It is for believers in
love, not for those who fear or dread. It is to be
a witness of Christ and to give Jesus testimony to
others and to give our walk to Jesus Christ. It is
a time to see our mistakes and to overcome them,
to see our successes and to celebrate. Everything
is possible in life. We should be free like in the
Camino, free from guilt, more forward. Don't be

afraid to live life! Christ awaits you with opened arms. He needs us to change this world individually. Never is later. It is never too late.. good camino! E-mail augustotriacastela@wanadoo.es.

After doing my laundry, which dried quickly in the sun, I prepared supper and ate with the Québecquois couple. Afterward, I went for a well-earned sleep, sharing my room with two college kids from the Midwest. The next morning I walked to the store and waited with a few others for a taxicab—a Spaniard with a sprained ankle and an older German woman with swollen feet; like me, they could no longer walk. In the cab, instead of going to the next town as I had plannned, I could not help but stop in the lovely town of Samos, which has an enormous monastery.

There, I had breakfast and waited until the monastery opened. I left my backpack in the café and observed the quiet little town. The monastery is quite large with a river flowing quietly nearby. Ducks were sitting on eggs next to the river, and stray dogs occasionally came to beg for food. Now the woman from Nova Scotia appeared. I had not seen her for quite a while, so we chatted a while before she continued on her way. Next, the two older French pilgrims arrived. It seemed they always argued like two old women. They, too, left after a snack. I stayed and admired the scenery.

The bridge near the monastery is beautiful, with ironwork full of scalloped designs. It was time for their tour. My guide, a young woman, took me on a walk through the big halls and chapels. There were only a handful of monks, which seemed a shame. At one time,

The monastery of Samos

this monastery must have had hundreds of monks, but now, like many other places, it lacked life. Many of the pilgrims come here, and some stay within its walls. However, they open their doors late, and most pilgrims do not want to wait around.

After sitting there for most of the day, I hitched a ride with some German tourists to the next town of Sarria. I walked slowly uphill to the albergue and gladly shed my backpack. The hostel already seemed packed when the gang gradually trickled in. I had supper as usual with the Brazilians, the Italians, and a group of Canadian women, all of whom were over seventy-six years of age. They told me, their secret: Walk only a few miles each day; we have all the time in the world, and what else are we going to do with it? Enjoy the wine!

Another rowdy evening—laughing and walking downhill through small streets of Triacastela to the Rio

Celerio walk, where there were many restaurants and people enjoying the evening. We feasted in one of the many cafés while the locals screamed at the world cup games on the large-screen television. I missed much of this historic town because of my difficulty with walking. We all retired for the evening, but the Australian girl who slept next to my bed was downstairs becoming even more rowdy, finally coming in around dawn, drunk as a skunk. She was a dentist taking a work break—or perhaps a breakdown.

I got up the next day and again took the bus to the next town, which gave me a new outlook on the towns. The bus did not follow the Camino, but went an alternate route through other little towns. Girls were going to school and we passed through villages and picked up older women who were going shopping. It was nice to see such lively towns. We do not see this while walking the Camino.

We passed beautiful soft mountains with forests and many farms. It is poor country, and one sees many women and men looking worn by work. They work hard keeping gardens and farms, raising families, taking care of husbands, and keeping house—all with a limited amount of money. Most women were short-legged and stocky with short waists, short hair, and no makeup. It is a life of hard work during the week, with prayers on Sunday in the numerous chapels and churches in the villages and countryside. Here it is definitely poorer than its neighboring state of Castile and León. I was thinking that the younger generation will certainly not tend the fields or settle into their mothers' roles. The younger ones dressed like teenagers everywhere—tight jeans,

Farmers at work in Galicia

belly button showing, no worries, and cell phones. What will become of the village life? Thanks to the influx of pilgrims who travels through the area by the thousand, some villages are doing very well. The landscape is beautiful from the bus; it is early morning, clouds are resting in the valley below, and the gentle hills are waking to the gentle rays of the sun. You could mistake some of these misty clouds for the sea.

I eventually arrived in the town of Portomarín and waited outside until the albergue opened. The usual gang showed up, and I went to the pharmacy to buy some anti-inflammatory cream. Nevertheless, I still cannot walk much. The region is beautiful; we had left the mountains for softer hills, rivers, and reservoir-lakes. I must come back through here to walk it.

I am sitting in the large dorm, there are about forty people, everyone talking, several languages, sleeping, resting, reading, sharing stories... it is difficult to be here because I have arrived by bus.. but I have no choice... my plane does not leave for several days, so I must do as if I was walking each section. The church in Portomarín is very different, like a box, a square, or a fortress. Built in the twelfth century, it is called Iglesia de San Juan o de San Nicolás.

This town was also influenced by the Knights of Saint John and the Templars, like many of the towns along the Camino. Tonight there is a service I planned to attend to get a feeling for the town, which is on a hill and surrounded by lakes and soft hills surrounding. Portomarín was rebuilt on higher ground, because the original town is now submerged in a reservoir built many years ago.

Inside, the church is sparse, and the service, as .it turns out, consisted of a prayer to the virgin and a small man reciting a litany to the Virgin in a high-pitched voice. It seemed as though he recited hundreds of expressions about the virgin. The church was full of tiny old women dressed in black, and he went on and on for at least half an hour. This special liturgy to the Virgin reminded me that the Camino is very much a Marian path, with many of the churches along the way dedicated to the Virgin. I view the Camino as a very feminine path, though many men walk it (as mentioned earlier concerning male and female, devotion to Mary gives birth to the female within the male, while the Christ engenders the male within the female).

Many pilgrims came to the service that evening, including a couple of older French men who had just finished telling stories full of sexual innuendos over a cup of coffee. As he left the second service, one of the French pilgrims' faces seemed transformed and purified. He looked relaxed and renewed; a remarkable transformation. It proves the strength with which litanies to the Virgin work on the pilgrims, who may or may not be aware of it. I wouldn't ask about that; it is private, and I may only observe.

The churches all have lovely little ancient, mummy-like old women sitting in their services. They go to help the lonely priest celebrate and preserve the ancient rites, and we Camino pilgrims benefit from their care and love. It gives us a wonderful way to celebrate after a day's walk when we attend. We leave, but the women remain behind to keep alive ancient Christian traditions. We headed for a late supper, and I bumped into the Italians again at a local restaurant. One person my age, a man from Rome, complained that he was lonely at home; his children had grown, and his big house was empty. There was also an Italian woman who was a pretty, forty-year-old with curly dark hair from northern Italy. My Italian artist and her boyfriend were getting quite drunk. It was a very warm evening and filled with the kind of enthusiasm that only the Italians can radiate—the sun itself comes from the Italian language.

The next morning, I took a bus once more to the next city. I stopped and had coffee and pastries, then headed toward Santiago on another bus. Along the way, I saw an old woman cutting hay by hand with a sickle. She wore a smock and a handkerchief on her head and was using a pitchfork to put the hay on a two-wheel cart, harnessed and pulled by a bullock, just as it has been done for hundreds of years. There were also cows in the fields and many gardens planted neatly with beautiful heads of lettuce, leeks, and lots of cabbage. The agriculture of Galicia includes vineyards and figs, but less than in the other provinces of Roja and Castile y León, which were far richer it seems.

Now we are going over hills and soft mountains with eucalyptus tree groves in this ancient land, adding another flavor to the scenery. It reminded me of Ecuador. It was pleasant to see the old people working and still part of the land and villages and drinking coffee, beer, or wine at the local cafés and bars. This is a country steeped in tradition. They have not yet suffered the death of soul, which may come with the next generation. It is a far more pleasant sight than the living cemetery of retirement for the elderly that one sees in the U.S.

❦

I would be able to spend three days in Santiago and stay in one place. My flight was scheduled for May 21, and it was the nineteenth. I arrived in the late morning and took a city bus to the center. Santiago was busy with pilgrims, tourists, and its normal business. I was walking and trying to find a place to stay, but I would not stay in the albergue, which is too far from the city center. A woman noticed that I was a pilgrim and told me she had a place to stay. I followed her thankfully and entered a small bed and breakfast full of English tourists. It was a flat with four tiny rooms, a kitchen, and bathrooms. This would be fine for me; it was not too expensive, and it would be the first time in six weeks that I would sleep in one place for more than one night and with less than eight to eighty people in a room. I was looking forward to this luxury. I shed my backpack and joyfully went into the famous city to pay my respects to St. James of Compostela.

I headed toward the Cathedral, which was very close, after wandering through the meandering streets with their many shops and restaurants filled with tourists, most of whom had no idea that some of us had walked so far to get here. To them, we must have looked like a bunch of slovenly, dirty-looking men and women. And they would have been right; by this time, our clothes were worn out and we look like we had been on the road, with our wind-burned and wrinkled faces, our baggy pants, and our dusty, well-used shoes. Moreover, some of us looked a bit lost in this huge city. Some of the pilgrims arrived directly at the cathedral with all their belongings in heavy backpacks, as well as ponchos, because it was raining.

Many wandered in the cathedral, which is enormous but not especially beautiful; the León and Burgos cathedrals were far more elaborate. The Cathedral of Santiago de Compostela is quite austere by Catholic standards. Nonetheless, everyone was touching the famous place, and some of the stones were well worn by the hundreds of years of pilgrims' hands.

After my visit to the cathedral, I returned to my room. It was nice to be alone after a month on the road and with such a huge new family still alive within me. I met dozens and dozens of pilgrim men and women, as well as those who not pilgrims, such as the ones who generously took care of our needs. As I think it now in this lonely little bedroom (I am writing this in the hills surrounding Florence), I see that we became friends, family, brothers, and sisters as we walked day by day. To the younger pilgrims, I became a mother, to other a confidante and a friend. To me, the camaraderie was the real Camino.

Many churches along the Camino had been closed, and after a long day on the road, some of us had just wanted to sit quietly in a church, but it was impossible. So we stopped in meadows of sweet-scented thyme, rosemary, sage and lavender to delight in nature—a field of poppies here, and beautiful stone wall there, an ancient fountain, or simply sitting outside a café in an old village visiting with our growing family. That was my true Christian pilgrimage—to meet everyone with openness, acceptance, a smile or laugh, understanding, and compassion, especially when the going got rough, both within and without.

I must say I had many laughs during those weeks. We all laughed while walking, and many times got lost through not paying attention. At the many stops along the way, we laughed at night before going to sleep and when getting up in the morning. We laughed at how sour we could be at times; these were wonderful baths of laughter. I encountered many wonderful and unforgettable faces from around the world—from Brazil, Mexico, Puerto Rico, New York City, California, Wisconsin, Bavaria, Germany, Switzerland, Norway, Iceland, Holland, Sweden, Denmark, France, Italy, Russia, Croatia, Austria, Hungary, Estonia, Australia, New Zealand, Japan, Venezuela, Chile and all over

In the large square near the Santiago Cathedral

Spain. Ranging from eighteen to seventy-eight years of age, rich and poor, professional and not, the Camino had been a borderless, multilingual community. To me it was Christianity at its best, regardless of the many religious denominations represented by the pilgrims. We slept together, sometimes like cattle; ate the same poor food; feasted or fasted; faced the same elements of winds, storms, rain, sun, cold; and walked the same hills, *mesetas,* mountains, valleys, and forest.

Many pilgrims return each year to experience this community of walking pilgrims and to be a part of the wave of people, rising each morning at six or seven o'clock and walking at least twenty kilometers or more every day toward Santiago.

Many of the pilgrims rarely or never go to church and are not very religious. Many are not Catholics but may be other types of Christians, though I found that many of the Protestants went to the Catholic services and accepted the Eucharist, as I did myself. It was an honor and showed respect to the often-lonely priests in the remote little villages when we went to the services and gratefully accepted their gift and dedication to helping us through their prayers.

I went to the Camino because I just simply love to walk. I went walking to rediscover my own voice, to bring some fresh air into my heart, and to give thanks to everyday and to every thing that crossed my path, whether scenery, plants, churches, people, or whatever.

All
And in return I received
All

I don't want anything in the world—I just like existing every minute and watching things coming and things going and then coming again, like storms and sunshine and then storms again. I don't want anything at all for the simple reason that I have everything, or rather, which is the same thing, everything has me. (Winifred Nicholson)[1]

🏵

Then my knee began to have a problem, and I had to be thankful for the pain as well. Perhaps it would not have been right not to experience real pain; this was, after all, not a vacation. Nevertheless, I had to walk with much pain, take buses, hitchhike, and take taxis, as well as walk to finish the trip. It gave me an opportunity to step out of the Camino, since I could no longer walk with the wave of friends. I saw them from the bus and I could see more of the whole picture. I was alone, as I am now with another group, as I did not start with these people; the ones I traveled with for four weeks were about three days behind, still on the Camino.

I slept well in my little room. I got up to have breakfast of tea and croissant, and then I went to the cathedral to get a good seat for the pilgrims' mass, which is celebrated everyday at noon. I sat in the front so I could see everything, and I am glad that I was early, because the cathedral suddenly seemed to fill up from all corners. I saw many pilgrims, some of whom had just arrived in Santiago, wet and tired but happy to be at the end of the long road, now shoving their backpacks into the corners. The cathedral is austere and without stained glass in its few windows. While it is simple inside, it still has many Vatican-like gold angels and gaudy sculptures to compensate.

---

1. In Astrid Fitzgerald, *An Artist's Book of Inspiration: A Collection of Thoughts on Art, Artists, and Creativity,* Great Barrington, MA: Lindisfarne Books, 1996.

The church was packed as the service was about to begin when a tiny nun shoved me aside and squeezed into the seat next to me. She was pleasant and smiled warmly at me. Seven priests celebrated this mass. It is moving for a non-religious spiritual person to be with hundreds of pilgrims who have walked so far to be at Finistere—"the end of the world," as people viewed it centuries ago.

The nun who sat next to me was dressed neatly in navy blue and prayed the whole time. As we were leaving, she gave me a kiss on the cheek, which pleased me very much. The singing was lead by another nun; we needed a nice strong chorus, but it was not there. When we received the Eucharist, there were so many of us that the priests spread out in all directions to meet the needs of the believers, most of whom are not practicing Catholics. However, it did not matter at that moment, because this seemed beyond religion; we had lived, slept, and eaten together; we had sweated, ached, showered, and sang together; now we feasted together.

Then a group of at least six or seven strong men who do this all the time took a hold of the long, thick ropes that carry the suspended incense burner and started to swing it around—up and up it went, almost touching the top of the basilica. The priests, who were generally there to see this spectacle, nevertheless took time to observe and delight in the magical, circus-like activity.

The incense wafted throughout the church. Incense changes the atmosphere in a church, and it is said that the spiritual beings partake in Christian ritual through the smoke that rises to meet them. It was a powerful moment, and it seemed that the apostle St. James must have been present in spirit in the church dedicated to him, especially with so many pilgrims who had just walked the Camino under his protection. The little nun next to me was laughing at my childish behavior. As the smell of the frankincense rose, the world of the invisible came to meet us and the organ played loudly as to awaken us to another reality. Rudolf Steiner had this to say about such experiences:

> Imagine a priest at the sacrificial altar in those ancient times when religion was based on true knowledge of spiritual laws. Imagine a priest kindling the flame, the smoke rising and actually becoming a sacrifice in that it is borne upward with prayers.
>
> What really happened in such sacrifices? The priest stood at the altar where the smoke was produced. There, where the solid emerged from the warmth, a spirit was enchanted, and, because a human being accompanied the process with prayers, the spirit was taken into the person and was released again when the human being died and entered into the higher world. What did the disciples of the ancient wisdom say to those who were to understand such a ritual? They explained that if you look at the external world so that your spiritual activity does not remain attached to the smoke, but rises spiritually to the fire element, then after death you free the enchanted spirit that dwells in the smoke. Those who had gained an understanding of the process would reply, "If the spirit that dwells in the smoke remains unchanged,

it will have to accompany me in a next incarna-
tion; after death it cannot return to the spiritual
world. But if I have released it, if I have led it back
to the fire, after my death it will rise into worlds
of spirit and no longer need to return to Earth at
my birth.".....

Through wisdom, which we develop within ourselves, we continually liberate elemental beings
when we die; but through lack of wisdom, through
materialistic attachment to the world of the senses,
we bind elemental spirits to us and force them
into this world to be reborn with us over and over
again.....

Human beings who are bright and cheerful, who
are satisfied with life and of a cheerful disposition because of their understanding of the world,
are continually liberating beings who are chained
because of the waning Moon. These beings enter
into such people, but are continually released
because of their serene soul disposition, inner
contentment, and harmonious view of life. Beings
who enter into us when we are sullen, peevish,
completely discontented, depressed, and pessi-
mistic remain in the condition of enchantment
in which they were at the time of the waning
Moon. There are human beings who, through the
fact that they have achieved a harmonious feeling about the world and a cheerful disposition,
work, in a wonderfully liberating way, on large
numbers of elementals, who come into being in
the way described. The human being, through

a harmonious perception of the world, through inner contentment with the world, frees spiritual elemental beings. Through moroseness, ill humor, and discontentment, a person imprisons elemental beings who could be freed through serenity....

If, through ill humor and hypochondria, a person leaves the spirits that had to be called into oneself for the order of the moon to be fulfilled, then these spirits remain bound to that person and must be born with him or her when the person enters a new existence. Thus we have a third kind of elemental spirits, which either are freed at the time of a person's death and return to their homeland, or which must enter this world again with the human being.[1]

✤

I was very grateful for this service, performed especially for us. At the end of the service, the priest in charge started to read the names and countries of all the pilgrims and from where they had begun, thus acknowledging their efforts. It was a wonderfully powerful moment to hear where the pilgrims had come from and how far they had traveled, coming from all across the world. We all felt thankful, as well as a strong fellowship with all the individuals who had ever walked the Camino. The presiding priest (or bishop) gave a

1. Rudolf Steiner, *The Spiritual Herarchies and the Physical World: Reality and Illusion,* Great Barrington: Anthroposophic Press, 1996, pp. 45–49.

nice speech in English, and in it he recognized that no one really knows why pilgrims are flocking to this path nowadays. He noted that 100,000 people come annually and that the reason is a mystery. It is not because of their religiousness or their Catholic faith, but an enigma.

Whereas monasteries are becoming obsolete and emptying, the modern nuns and monks (us) had taken to the road from all over the world. It reminded me of my practice of Vipassana as taught by Goenka; on the Camino I attained the same state as when I was practicing the noble path of Buddhist Vipassana (insight meditation) during my late twenties. Then, we had sat for ten days in silence—the opposite of the Camino. In the practice of Vipassana, we were separated, with men on one side and women on the other. On the Camino, we sleep close to people we have never met, men and women; we have cell phones, books, internet, and whatever we want to bring. On the Camino, the senses are wide opened, but in Vipassana we close the senses for the ten days. We were not drinking, of course, and eating vegetarian food. We had wine every night, however, on the Camino, and parties at night when we are not too tired. We had endless conversations and shared meals and snacks at all times of the day.

Even with all that freedom on the Camino, however, most were celibate, but freely, not by force. We accepted one another for who we are—farmers, doctors, students, police officers, gardeners, homemakers, business people, linguists, lovers, poets, dentists, writers, monks, oil magnates, priests, bums, and so on. We learned to put up with one another. Our reasoning was put to the test;

we walked in the company of people who probably would not be our companions at home. We all walked the same path with more or less the same baggage on our backs—young people who have pierced their bodies everywhere, old men, fat men, skinny women, old women, matrons, beautiful Mary-like young women, little old ladies, young men, adventurers, Don Juans, lonely women, priests. We were all human being, sharing the same path for days, weeks, or months, sometimes mere hours, then returning home with a heart full of well-lived moments and memories of sharing love and care, the surroundings. It was in this way that we sent wonderful energy into Northern Spain and into the world's atmosphere, so that even after thousands of years it will continue to shine brightly.

> Those whose thoughts have become living forces within them through their meditation are living in the divine stream...

> Those who engage in true meditation are living in a process that is, at the same time, a world process. What takes place is this: In meditation, warmth is consumed and, therefore, cold ensues; the universal ether is cooled. In addition, since light, too, is consumed, it is dimmed and darkness ensues. It is always possible for a clairvoyant to tell if one has meditated in a particular place; a shadow-image of that person remains behind, which is, in fact, cooler than its surroundings. Something has been affected, which one may compare with a photographic print.

If we reflect on this, we can understand how some-one can return to earth and a new earthly life and still finds traces of one's meditation thoughts in the cosmic ether. Here we have the concrete example of the way karma works. The meditator increasingly feels that it has become more than one's own thoughts; something transpires, into which you are placed of course, but it continues outside as something that remains. One feels oneself, as it were, within the atmosphere of the weaving and being of one's thoughts, as though thoughts move through us as waves, and it gives us a certain feeling. It is the assurance that one stands in a spiritual world as oneself, but also as a member weaving in the overall weave of the divine world. A remarkable feeling then comes to us in the stillness of the soul: it is not created by you alone—it is created. You have begun to stir these waves, but they spread themselves around you. They have a life of their own and you are but the center.[1]

Sitting in the cathedral, I felt the same as I had at the end of our Buddhist retreats; my senses were height-ened, but by completely different means. I was lead to the same place, one of fellowship and freedom. Many

1. Rudolf Steiner, *Guidance in Esoteric Training: From the Eso-teric School,* London: Rudolf Steiner Press, 2001, p. 169 (transla-tion revised).

roads lead to the same land, and the sooner we learn this, the sooner we will find peace.

It is easier to talk to the angels after spending so many days on the road, amid such beauty and in the company of wonderful human beings. I think that here they can listen to us a little more, be happy for what we are doing, and even send us some messages about our destiny. Rudolf Steiner imagines it this way:

> The stars once spoke to humanity
> But it is the fate of the world
> That the stars are silent now,
> To feel the silence
> Can be painful for human beings.
>
> But in the deepening silence
> The word that human beings can speak to the
>   stars
> Is ripening:
> To become aware of that Word
> Can strengthen the human spirit.[1]

When we get closer to the spiritual world, we can speak to the stars, and in turn we can help this world. Through the many thousands who come to the Camino, this will make a difference. We are breathing life into what Owen Barfield described so aptly in his *History in English Words*: "Today cold stars glitter unapproachable overhead, and with a naïve detachment, mind watches matter moving incomprehensibly in the void. At last, after four centuries, thought has shaken herself

---

1. Rudolf Steiner, in Christopher Bamford, *An Endless Trace: The Passionate Pursuit of Wisdom in the West,* New Paltz, NY: 2003, p. 180.

free.[1] Now we are ensouling them again. "The great things of the world are not born in noise and tumult, but in intimacy and stillness."[2]

I spent the afternoon in a nice coffee and tea room, in which a number of Spaniards, looking very intellectual, were using laptops or reading the newspapers, along with a myriad of strange-looking pilgrims, who were busily writing postcards and catching up with their loved ones and just happy (or perhaps unhappy) to have arrived finally at their destination. I just enjoyed the coffee and reading and watching people pass by. Later, I returned to my room and had a peaceful night's rest.

I got up the next morning quite early, wishing to get a seat up front again for the mass. This time I chose to sit to one side so that I could observe the incense flying across the side of the church. I arrived by ten o'clock, and an hour later the church was almost filled, with still another hour until mass would begin. At this point, familiar pilgrims' faces began to appear. The Dutch man from The Hague sat beside me. It was 300 kilometers back when I had last seen him. We had a conversation about Buddhism and the reason why people do not go to church.

I noticed a lovely face just to the left, one row ahead. It was the Hungarian doctor Eva, sitting with her son. She found it hard to believe that we ended up here at the same time. I had last seen her 490 kilometers back on the Camino, and she was very emotional to

1. Owen Barfield, *History in English Words,* Great Barrington, MA: Lindisfarne Books, 2002, p. 143.

2. Rudolf Steiner, *The Temple Legend: Freemasonry and Related Occult Movements*, London: Rudolf Steiner Press, 1988, .p. 279.

be there with her son. She was a pilgrim who had been supported by her whole community, which gave her a going-away party. Her community had remained in her thoughts throughout the pilgrimage—only an eastern, Slavic soul could feel so deeply and take the pilgrimage so seriously. In the fervent, serious faith visible on their faces, I could see that Eastern Europe is very different from the West. They lived every sacred word.

Meeting these people again, with whom I had walked what seemed like so long ago, was more than a surprise—perhaps fate. The Camino is full of such stories. We meet the people we are supposed to meet, no more, no less. We are all called to be here, we heard the message, and we walked toward one another, pass one another, walk together, disappear, meet again, and say goodbye ... until next time we meet.

The Hungarian's son had flown in from Budapest to be with his mother at the end of her journey, and they were going to spend a week traveling around before returning to Hungary.

Next I saw the couple from Texas and California; they were planning to go to a beach in Southern Spain. The couple had walked with me from the very beginning. The Italians, Brazilians, and others were still on the road, and I thought about them because it was raining very hard. They would be walking in pouring rain on a cold and muddy path and would not arrive until the next day, when I would be flying off to London and on to Chicago. I had not said goodbye, but they would have a place in my heart forever.

The Cathedral was now packed. It was resounding and filled with human emotions, and again the priest acknowledged that the phenomena of pilgrims on the Camino was growing quickly, with many thousands coming each year. He recognized and affirmed what all of us had experienced on the Camino—that we do not often know one another's language, and speak instead with the heart in the new language we are learning. Perhaps that is all that we needed to learn.

Following the service, we said good bye and all went our separate ways. I went back to my favorite café and spent the afternoon chatting with various pilgrims. Then, as I was sipping that wonderful drink, it occurred to me that I had not really finished my conversation with the Dutch man about Buddhism and that I needed to share with him some of my experiences on that path. I felt bad that I had not finished what I wanted to say to him.

I packed up my stuff and walked out of the café, and whom do I meet at the door? It was the Dutch man! Who needs a telephone? We made a date to have supper together later, which turned out to be a three hour dinner during which we finished discussing the serious projects that he was doing, our life-changing experiences, and about his lovely wife, who understood that he needed this time by himself to consider his writings. It was a mutual sharing of interests in spiritual matters. Because this is the Camino, these things happens regularly; it is magic and only requires living in the moment. This was happening to everyone I met. We were connected at very deep levels; a phone was unnecessary for most of us. When you have access to the world of living, etheric forces, you recognize that those forces are the opposite of the earth's gravitational forces: gravity = selfishness; antigravity = selflessness

When you begin to use the *language of the heart,* it functions at a different level, and as we experienced it, the language is instantaneous. Here the word *selfishness* must be wiped off the map; it kills this new language instantly. As all journeys must end I will end with these words:

> An artist must educate himself, he cannot be educated, he must test things out as they apply to himself; his life is one long investigation of things and his own reaction to them. If he is to be interesting to us it is because he renders a very personal account....

> The best art the world has ever had is but the impress left by men who have thought less of making great art than of living fully and completely with all their faculties in the enjoyment of full play. From these the result is inevitable. (Robert Henri)[1]

1. In Astrid Fitzgerald, *An Artist's Book of Inspiration: A Collection of Thoughts on Art, Artists, and Creativity,* Great Barrington, MA: Lindisfarne Books, 1996, pp. 196–197.

About the Author

MARIE-LAURE VALANDRO WAS BORN in 1948 in Tunisia and lived in Dijon, France, until the age of seven, when her family moved to Morocco and Algeria during the revolutionary years. At age eleven she returned with her family to France before moving to Boston four years later, where she received her B.A. in secondary education in the Romance languages and literature, and her M.A. in modern languages, literature, and drama.

Marie-Laure studied and earned a black belt in karate and gained an understanding of qi (life forces) from her Okinawan master. She taught high school in Boston before moving to Paris at twenty-three and furthering her studies at Sorbonne and began visiting sacred Christian sites in Europe. She taught in Paris and Vermont and then moved to Tehran in 1974, where she taught technical English for several years and backpacked around the world between teaching assignments. After encountering Buddhism, she studied Vipassana meditation with Master Goenka in Québec, England, and India.

While living in the Moslem world, Ms. Valandro studied Sufism, Zoroastrianism, and the Qur'an as practiced in the villages. After traveling throughout the East, she met her husband in Iran, had a child while in Vermont, and then, during the Ayatollah Khomeini's regime, returned to Tehran so that her husband could meet their son. She left after a year, refusing to raise her son in a dictatorship. Later, her husband left Iran, and they moved to New Hampshire, where they had a daughter.

Marie-Laure quit teaching and began studying Anthroposophy full time, while also working as a translator from French to English. At this point, she returned to painting, which had been abandoned in college. She met the art therapist Liane Collot d'Herbois in Holland, who guided her in establishing the Liane Collot d'Herbois Therapeutic Painting School in Wisconsin, the only training of its kind in the U.S.

Marie-Laure is an avid traveler and gardener.

www.ingramcontent.com/pod-product-compliance
Lightning Source LLC
Chambersburg PA
CBHW022131080426
42734CB00006B/314